ROSEANNE
on
Fantasy Men:

Anyway, so Woody Allen and I become friends and everything and we call each other on the phone all the time, but he calls me more than I call him and talks over his ideas for movies and stuff. Then, of course, he realizes that I am the most brilliant woman on earth at this time, and that it is me and me alone who can really save the world. Then of course I do away with nuclear weapons and war and violence, and everyone lives happily ever after, and everyone loves, adores and worships me.

Then I dump him for Mel Gibson, who I meet after dark behind an old warehouse, and well, you know . . . Mel had very little flesh left on his bones a short while later.

ROSEANNE
MY LIFE AS A WOMAN

Roseanne Barr

Harper Paperbacks

Harper & Row, Publishers, New York
Grand Rapids, Philadelphia, St. Louis, San Francisco
London, Singapore, Sydney, Tokyo, Toronto

In some instances, names have been changed.

Harper Paperbacks a division of Harper & Row, Publishers, Inc.
10 East 53rd Street, New York, N.Y. 10022

A hardcover edition of this book was published in 1989 by
Harper & Row, Publishers, Inc.

Cover photo © 1989 by Lynn Goldsmith

First Harper Paperbacks printing: October 1990

Printed in the United States of America

HARPER PAPERBACKS and colophon are trademarks
of Harper & Row, Publishers, Inc.

10 9 8 7 6 5 4 3 2 1

For my Sister, Geraldine, for being intense, passionate, committed, brilliant, fierce—for creating a large part of me, my career, the world. Where do you end, where do I begin? You believed in me always, as I believe in you. Many of the words in this book come from you, and I look forward to your book, your film. The world is waiting for you, Sister.

ACKNOWLEDGMENTS

Jessica, Jake, Jennifer—for being the best inspirations and young humans there are.

Brandi—welcome home!

Gail—you did a great job!

Craig Nelson—thanks for the encouragement!

Stephanie—for understanding a sister Scorpio.

Rick—for hearing and counseling.

Maxine—for sharing.

Tom—for making me laugh and knowing what it means,

and

to the memory of Woman to Woman Bookstore,
where all the books lived.

Thank you to these people I learned from:

Mae West	*Ethel Merman*
Dorothy Parker	*Judy Holliday*
Martha Ray	*Bette Midler*
Fanny Brice	*Rusty Warren*
Carol Channing	*Millie Jackson*
Carol Burnett	*Bette Davis*
Lucy	*Marjorie Main*
Lily Tomlin	*Marilyn*
Phyllis Diller	*Gilda*
Joan Rivers	*Moms Mabley*
Vivian Vance	*Gracie Allen*
Pearl Bailey	*Barbra Streisand*
Renee Taylor	*Elaine May*
Anne Meara	*Selma Diamond*

Thank you also:

Lenny	*Richard Pryor*
Dick Gregory	*Rodney*
Leonard Barr	*Jackie Vernon*
Johnny Carson	*Steve Allen*
Lord Buckley	*John Belushi*

PREFACE

Ms Barr, your book is a celebrity autobiography, isn't it? Did you use a ghost writer?

No, I wrote it myself. I don't believe it is a celebrity autobiography, actually.

No? How so?

It's a book about *celebrity.*

So, it's some kind of an expose?

No, it's about becoming.
It's a book about being Jewish in America.
It's a book about the sixties.
It's a book about the women's movement.
It's a book about the left
     two sisters
     Motherhood
     dysfunctional childhood
     women

upward mobility
denial
a religious experience that changed
    a life
a commitment to spiritual Belief
a commitment to a political ethic
sex, food, rock & roll
subtext—with the same stories told in
    various ways
comedy
goals
self-help
men/women
the power of books
the power of positive thinking
corporate think
Exile
God
Patriarchy
Matriarchy

INTRODUCTION

I am quite alone today, my deadline fast approaching, the day I'm required to turn in this pitiable manuscript that masquerades as my life's story. I used to think I was an interesting person, but I must tell you how sobering a thought it is to realize your life's story fills about thirty-five pages and you have, actually, not much to say.

I don't know why in the name of God I ever decided that I had anything to say or write. I thought it was so easy, I thought I had so very many droll stories to tell that would doubtless capture the bored imaginations of throngs of readers. Well now I feel like an idiot and a fool, and I don't know which is worse. I must be about the most dull person on earth, since I only have a mere forty pages of life to tell.

I was born in Salt Lake City and grew up there amongst Mormons as a Jewish girl. That's about four lousy pages . . . do you believe it? To think that all those years I told myself, just to live through the onslaught (considering Mormons, as I do, to be a sort of Nazi Amish, a people who have made the tragic mistake of thinking that style can be substituted for substance, to whom drinking, dancing, and the pleasures of the flesh are the very worst sins on earth) that someday I would write about it—I must have said that to myself a million times. And now after thirty-five years, it comes out to four lousy pages. What am I doing?

Then I realize that most people can't even *spell* correctly, and feel cheered. My Hubby volunteered to take the three younguns camping over this weekend so that I could attempt to hammer out some meager little words on my new Smith Corona. Everyone who is modern tells me to get a word processor as it would make my chore so much easier, and I thought about it, but can't see any of my favorite writers (Poe, Thomas, Woolf, Stein, Bukowski) in front of a word processor, and anyway, I have a deep and abiding mistrust of computers and technology, because I read somewhere that they cause cancer and throw off some sort of a zap that can turn you soul-dead.

Anyway, Hubby was so excited to be able to go camping, since I never go. We used to go a lot back in the days when I used to think that communing with nature was a healing, positive thing. Now, I think I'd like to commune with other things—like room service and temperature control. Bill is such an outdoorsy kind of a guy . . . very Irish, very Celtic, very *Whole Earth Catalog.* He loves nothing more than hiking up hills in combat boots, building fires and cooking bacon, unrolling smelly sleepy bags, telling scary stories, sleeping on top of mother earth, and breathing in the scent of pine needles. I used to be like that, too, and now am wondering what happened to change it. My children are like their father, like most children probably are, loving to get dirty, loving life with no walls.

I don't enjoy relaxing at all anymore; it bores me. I like to, instead, live the Type-A high-stress existence of the eighties that comes from watching TV and feeling my temples begin to throb, blood coursing through my veins, which now stand out from my neck, and swearing, saying things like "TV sucks" then going into my high-tech kitchen, heating up delivered pizza in a modern microwave, going back to the couch, using the remote control to run through all eighty-six channels, saying at each change . . . "this is all shit, it's all shit." Then, turning off the TV and plugging in my Nintendo cartridges and attempting to save that goddam princess for at least twenty minutes, then swearing and saying "I'm going to call my sisters up."

Of course, neither of my sisters are ever home, as they are both newlyweds and like newlyweds must either be having l'amour (d'amour?), or be out searching for fun things to share with their respective partners. It makes me feel just the teensiest bit nostalgic then, back to the days when Bill and I would do things just to experience them together. God, gag me. But because they are modern sisters, they have answering machines, and so I can leave horrible messages on them. Then I can go back to the typewriter and write two words down and say, "I need to wait till it's dark, I write better then." Then I go into town to look at a coffee table, because I can never find a good one.

I hired somebody when I first got this house

to redecorate it for me . . . then she told me what she estimated the bill would be. Bill said "Why don't you just do it yourself? I've always loved the way you fixed up every place we've lived." But this is California, I said, my taste just won't do here. Nothing is supposed to look cozy and cluttered (the way I like it!) here. Everything here has to look like New Mexico. But then I decided that I hate pine furniture covered in white muslin, and I hate cactuses, and I hate bleached wood. So, I did it myself. I got huge floral prints and wooden cupboards and my house looked like the Waltons's, my favorite TV show of all time.

Didn't you just love the Waltons? This mythical American family, who, in a departure for TV, were not all incredibly attractive? In fact their oldest son was a wimp with a big mole on his cheek, and the dad was an alcoholic in his final decline, and the mom later had to, after widowhood, I guess, move to cable TV and become a nurse, and the Grandpa was a leftover W.O.B.B.L.Y., a refugee from left-wing politics who personally knew Woody Guthrie, and the Grandma was a healer, a witch, a crone (who mixed poultices and teas), and they lived in a beautiful place, Walton's Mountain, and they were not racists or Jew haters (incredible) and all of their furniture was upholstered in flowery materials and everything else was wood?

And John Boy was going to grow up and be a writer. And everyone respected him for it, making him a bit of the family demi-god. Not like in a real family, like when you say you're going to be a writer, and your parents laugh at you and torment you by telling you, "What you really need to do is get a husband" (like mine did when I would always say I was going to be a writer), and act like you got bugs in the brain like, you're actually mentally ill, because you would want to do something you loved, something that was creative, and why should *you* get to do that, when both of them wanted to be writers too, and had to settle for being machinists and secretaries?

The world lost two very good writers, my parents, when, in its laconic Kismet, it stuck them in Salt Lake City, Utah, and forced mortgages and time payments on them, so that the daily grind of the paycheck forced them to give up their dreams. So I'm a product of mixed signals and double messages because my parents taught me on the one hand to dream Dreams. They encouraged me to write plays for the neighborhood kids to put on, and even helped me create the plays, and then they would tell me it was impossible to be a dreamer, an artist, a writer, the world would not allow it.

Yet, on certain nights my parents would tell stories. Daddy had his special stories and Mom had hers. They would be so excited to have new people come over, people who had never heard their stories before, usually brought to our house by those who already *had* heard the stories.

The new people who came with the seasoned people, and the seasoned people, would sit on the couches, and Mom and Dad would be on the loveseat.

We kids were running in and out, looking at the people on the couches, and then run into Mom and Dad's bedroom and talk about how ugly, stupid, and dumb the guests were.

Mom would begin by hostessing, chatting politely, drawing the newcomers in. When they were sufficiently comfortable, she would ask Daddy, to *please* tell the story about "The Barr Specialties Company" (a business that Daddy, his father and mother and Mama ran in SLC).

So Daddy would act, just for a few seconds, like he didn't wanna tell it. Everyone would say, "C'mon, Jerry!" and then he would say, "Ah, alright. Jesus, how'd did that go again? Oh, yeah."

Before I tell the story, I must say how I stood, near the door, every week, and watched my parents. Daddy was a great actor, I thought, because he did the same thing every time. Mama was great, too, because she would be his perfect Ed McMahon. When the audience was too blown away, Mama would say, "Can you believe he did that? I don't know about you, Barr." That would be the tension breaker, and shortly after the tension breaker everyone would leave. The tension breaker would come at different times each week, too. If Daddy and Mom only got to tell a few stories before the visitors would let their minds, and eyes, wander and act bored or terrified, Mom and Dad would remark afterward, "What boring, stupid people."

But, if the visitors stayed alert, inquisitive, and entertained, long enough for all four of Daddy's favorite stories (and then three or four of Mama's stories), they would remark afterwards, "What lovely, nice people. Let's invite them for dinner."

One story was about the time when our neighbor Jack came over to our house for dinner, and while we were all sitting at the table, he would chew and then spit out his food on the plate—like nothing was odd about that. (I remember this incident, too.) Daddy would say how shocked we were, etc., and how Mama made him clean up the plate, and throw it away.

Then there was the one about how Uncle Luke thought Coca-Cola Inc. was trying to make him confess that he took the Lindbergh baby, by shining bottle caps in his eyes. Then he'd say, "But I didn't take the Lindbergh baby."

Then there was the one about Uncle Larry painting everything in his home black, including himself, with a spray gun.

Then there was the one about how Grandpa sold all of the Mexicans and Catholics 3-D pictures of Jesus. How he sold all of them holy water fonts and blankets. How the gypsies thought Grandpa was a holy man, and would ask him to bless them, and then one day a lady asked Dad, "Why your father a Greek, but you a Jew" and Daddy said "I converted." Daddy would then tell about how Grandpa, his father, was the greatest con-man of all time and how he was an alcoholic, and how he was an atheist and a Bolshevik, in SLC. How he had died at birth in Kiev, but his grandmother took him in the kitchen and put him in the warm oven, and he turned pink and cried. And how Grandpa would then go down to skid row once a month, pick up a drunk, buy him new clothes, take him home to his family and buy them one week's worth of groceries, bless them, and then tell Daddy to tell those bastard Mormons, "This is my religion." Grandpa Sam had a deep admiration for Jesus because he was just one Jewish guy—and he took over the world.

After Daddy finished his stories, Mom would begin to tell hers. Her stories and style were different from Daddy's, told in the style of Midrash, a story that has both schmaltz and morals, one that usually ended the same way that it would begin.

Mom would tell how her mother Bobbe Mary would fight off ex-tenants, usually pissed-off men who would try to break down her doors and smash in her windows to try to get their rent deposits refunded. Mom would demonstrate how Bobbe Mary, hobbling on her cane and wearing her coke-bottle lenses, would beat the men up, never backing down, until they left or the cops came.

Mama's storytelling act usually included her favorites like:

- That I was born face first. The doctor said it seemed to him that I was quite anxious to get out there and see what was going on; Gawd if I had only known then what I know now I would have leapt from the womb and ran swiftly away into the night with the thought of perhaps finding a she-wolf to suckle me and keep me in her den where I would never have to face the possibility of any benefit lunches or interviews by disc jockeys.
- When Mother's father was in the house, in the final stages of cancer, and he, like many men to follow him, was totally enamored with my charms. While Mother and her mother were in the bedroom, caring for him, yours two-year-old truly took her tender and fat ass out to the busy streets and

the neighbor lady called Mother and shrieked "Get outside, quick, little Rosie is directing traffic." Mother ran because, I'm sure, they didn't have good health insurance and there I was, standing in the middle of the street with one chubby hand outstretched and the other waving to this man to go around me. The man, like many men to follow him, didn't get me at all, and found my humor to be—lax. Mother spanked me, and tells me that when her father found out that little Little Rosie had been abused he told her, "If I could only get out of this bed, I'd break both your legs." Although my grandpa died a short while later, I have always felt him hovering around, encouraging me to be as charming and adorable as I could possibly be. I love to tell stories about people who love me.

• When I was five years old and we lived across the street from a little grocery store, and Mother allowed me to go over there all by myself (which meant, of course, that she would stand there, and make sure all the traffic had subsided, and then, like a track coach, scream alright, go! and while I was going she would scream run! run! like it was the end of the world. I did not cross a street without her until I was nine years old).

When I came back and handed Mother her purchase she noticed I'd been given $1 too much in change, and decided to educate me as to the wise and crucial ways of being honest and god-fearing and right thinking and all, but because it was very cold outside, I refused to go back. Mother then drilled into me that our heavenly father was watching and would like it if I took back the dollar. Thus properly induced into religious ecstasy, turning to return the excess loot, I slipped on the ice and all of my upper teeth went cleanly and fully through my lip; I was rushed to the hospital, laid on a table, covered with a sheet from head to toe and underwent ninety minutes of surgery.

The wonderful lesson about honesty and doing the right thing was planted into my consciousness. I learned that not even God himself likes ASS KISSERS.

Even when very young, I knew that I would be the one person in a long ravaged line of storytellers, of persons with notebooks and drawers and cupboards and old cardboard boxes full of handwritten tales that would make it out of poverty and resignation, to be a writer.

I was invented by all these people, these writers and storytellers, and I love them, like John Boy loved his family, and that's why I love the Waltons so much.

ROSEANNE
MY LIFE AS A WOMAN

CHAPTER

1

Sometime after I was born in Salt Lake City, Utah, all the little babies were sleeping soundly in the nursery except for me, who would scream at the top of my lungs, trying to shove my whole fist into my mouth, wearing all the skin off on the end of my nose. I was put into a tiny restraining jacket to keep my hands away from the wounds.

My mother is fond of this story because to her it illustrates what she regards as my gargantuan appetites and excess anger. I think I was probably just bored.

Six months old. How *dull* everything is. Aunts and uncles would attempt to amuse me by making silly faces at my crib. I remember thinking "what assholes."

My grandmother did not bore me, though, because she smelled like bread and pickles.

When I was barely able to walk, uncles would jump out from behind things and scream "boo" at me. I always knew they did this for their own amusement, and recall wondering why they would want to debase themselves for the attentions of a tiny child. I would laugh, however, as this would quiet them.

What I liked to do was sit by myself, chewing and gnawing on various things. I liked eating pennies the very best, with their coppery and cool taste. . . . I would crawl all over the floor to find a fallen penny, but no sooner did I get the delicious thing into my mouth than some hardened adult would rip it from me.

I hated when my grandpa would throw me in the air and catch me. I remember worrying about his failing eyesight and growing senility, and praying that it would not cause him to forget that I was airbound and leave me to land upon my head—making me act in a manner appropriate to those living in Utah.

I would wear my cowgirl outfit with boots and a rope and a hat and a vest with a fringe, and invent little baby plays for myself, which always ended with me saving the world, a chore I have always known was my ultimate destiny.

Alas for me (and probably the world) I was so adorable that those larger than myself would carry me away from my purpose into a room furnished with adults—those people that I still find it almost impossible to identify with.

Then, as now, my greatest joy was to be all by myself where I could marvel at how much I knew about everything on earth.

My grandmother, Bobbe Mary, was the one adult I adored, because she encouraged my need to be the center of all creation. Always asking me what did I want to eat: bagels with chicken fat and salt, or challah with chicken fat and salt, or chicken soup with chicken fat and salt.

Chicken fat (or shmaltz) which to this day I still lust for in my heart (but like most progressive-minded Jews I eschew for health reasons—as well as assimilation). I resent that little wimp Nathan Pritikin for ruining it for all of us.

I liked to watch TV with Bobbe, I would sit at her feet in front of her chair, now in my bedroom, which I always regarded as the throne of the matriarchs, and watch her favorite show, "the EDZ OFF NIET" while she would give the play-by-play to me in a Lithuanian accent as thick as her shmaltz . . . "DZat no gud Jesse will be gitten vuts cummin to her sun enoff."

When not watching TV, she would tell me stories, using various parts of my anatomy as pigs or people in a steeple. To this day, I still enjoy imagining my fingers to be people . . . some nails are long (the ruling classes) and others I bite until stubby, they being the proletarian workers, bowlers, etc. They all look different when held up to the light. My husband calls this my pitty patting and yells at me to knock it off when he feels I'm being too obsessive. My dad used to get up out of his chair when I was younger and walk over to me and hit me upside the head, "Get your fingers out of your mouth!" and then go back to his chair where he would attack his fingernails (or I should say the remnants of what were once possibly fingernails).

I did not like living with my parents, even as a young child, because our house did not smell like bread and pickles, it smelled like nail polish.

When I was two, Mother took a job as a Dee's Hamburger Drive Inn cashier, and instead of letting me stay with Bobbe, she and Daddy thought putting me with other children would be a positive experience. In nursery school I was charmed with the unprecedented notion of being able to share myself and my space with persons of the same height. Disgusted by their foul odors and careless personal habits, I have burned in my memory Georgie who peed his pants and sat next to me everyday at lunch time. There were others who ate their boogers and laughed when someone farted. I found it tedious and would have preferred to discuss Hitler's invasion of Poland.

It was while being forced to play silly little games of ring around the rosey and such that I viewed my first male sexual organ because the bathrooms were co-ed. No penis envy; I thought his guts fell out of his vagina. Mother explained to me later that boys have "IT" so they could be Daddies and girls have theirs so they could be Mommies. Having no idea what any of that meant I thought Daddies were the walking wounded and that is why they had to sit around and be pampered and served—because they were handicapped.

After I refused to go back to school my new babysitter was Robbie, a huge Appalachian who lived in the apartment house with us. She wore overalls and chewed tobacky, which in the early 1950s in Salt Lake City meant that she was something of a social misfit. She called me Lil Bit. At that time, I was wearing casts on both legs, to correct my archless feet. The Utah pediatrician who recommended this I now think of as practicing ethnocide; Jews are entitled to flat feet. To this day I'm crazy about Jews who cut off their noses, change their names, starve off their Jewish fat, and then talk about how proud they are to be Jewish.

Anyway, because of those casts, Robbie would carry me everywhere and sing hillbilly songs to me. When I asked her what she was chewing on, she told me that it was black licorice. We would go up to her apartment every afternoon, and because she was a misfit, she had Elvis records. Robbie would cut a rug as she called it, to "Hounddog" and I enjoyed watching her dance.

She would also take me to Liberty Park where I would hobble around on my casts, which mother had painted green in order to cheer me up, and she would tell me the various names of the flowers and plants in the park. She would also tell me that nothing was really wrong with my legs or feet, but my parents needed to go see a psychie-latrist. I swore her my allegiance.

Thank all the gods for the women like Robbie, my babysitter . . . possessed of some sinister wisdom common only to those who are in league with our Mother the Earth. Those common people who know how to cure "ills" by going outside, picking a plant and boiling it into a tea that works faster and better than all the medication the FDA will ever approve.

I remember when those bad little girls Joanne and Binky said their mom told them that Robbie chewed tobacco like a man and was a crazy old bitch. I pulled myself up to my full two-year-old height, and becoming the Amazon Warrior I was destined to become, I called down the moon and yelled "Don't you ever call MY ROBBIE a bitch!" They ran home dragging their little tails behind them, honey.

Robbie proudly related this story to everyone in the neighborhood for weeks, "Lil Bit here told them girls she don't cotton to no ignernt folk bein' mean to her old Robbie."

In the end, looking back, I realize that I have molded myself after Robbie and Bobbe, one-half Tennessee Hillbilly, and one-half Jewish Matriarch.

CHAPTER

2

My grandmother (or Bobbe, as we say in the Jewish trade) came over to America from Lithuania when she was sixteen. She came here, not only like so many others because of the streets "being paved with gold" and all, but because she wanted to leave the place where the streets were paved with people who had not gone to America.

She was a widow of independent means. She owned her own apartment house in Salt Lake City and, after her husband died, ran it for many years alone.

Going over to her house was the most wonderful experience in the world for me. She always kept her door open, and the screen door latched. It was latched with a very rusty hook and eye–like contraption. You would stand outside on the little porch and yell "Bubs," and she would come and unlock the screen and let you in. Later, we learned how to pound on the outside door in just the right spot, and the latch would spring open. She kept the screen door locked so that the assorted drunks and ex-tenants seeking their damage deposits could not just wander in. In the worst of the inner-city neighborhoods there, on 6th East and 6th South, that rusty little hook did keep them all out. That, and perhaps the ornate jade mezuzah hung by the door.

You came here for tea, refuge, conversation, warmth, a game of gin rummy (which she always won); you came here to snoop in the closets (where she stored the wine she made herself from her grape arbor in the backyard), you came for a bagel, or soup, or to steal quarters out of her purse, to play in the junked cars she had in her backyard, or to go through the sheds, the wooden sheds back there that held furniture, and to the rear, held crates marked "Jewish Relocation Committee," crates that brought over the meager belongings of those who had survived the Germanic invasion of Judaism.

She had plants everywhere, untamed, greens and yellows, some pots full of browned and dead plants which she continued to water. I swear that the next time you looked at them, they were green again.

I loved my grandmother more than any other human being because she never lied, never told you what you wanted to hear, never compromised. She had a healthy hatred for all living human beings, all systems of government, all religion, except her own, of course, which was based on her intolerance of humanity with a little Judaism thrown in.

One of her great talents was her cooking, which consisted of exciting things to do with fats . . . she made a salad that was so incredible, and her spaghetti is still, to this day, untopped. You were never allowed in the cooking process, only to follow her and clean up, or chop walnuts, or peel potatoes. Bobbe would never give away her recipes, even to me or my sisters. We would help her cook, and try to watch, but, always, as we retrieved a spoon or a plate, some ingredient had been added, and if we asked, she would say, "Never mind."

We would go to Bobbe's house almost every day, and she would make us that incredible salad that came served in a bowl that had big green flowers on it, and she would put it onto a matching plate, with a "nice" glass of orange juice. Everything to Bobbe was "nice." A nice piece of fruit, a nice tomato, a nice bowl of soup. If we were very lucky, she would serve us spaghetti from a big pot on the stove. You would fight your siblings for the tarnished metal fork with the black handle that was about a hundred years old with two metal screws in the base of it, because the weight of that fork was perfect to eat with.

Afterward, as you were playing her a game of gin rummy with the radio turned to KALL talk station, both of you would keep your ears open, listening for the callers who made anti-Semitic statements. You'd hear one, the game would stop, Bobbe would call the station, who expected her, and set them all straight. If you were winning at gin, she would say "Go get the doorbell." "I didn't hear nuthin'" you'd say. "What are you, crazy? Someone is here to pay the rent!" So, you would go, and no one would be there. You would come back to the table, pick up your cards, and miraculously, the card she picked was gin! That was one of the hard lessons we had to learn. My sister still claims she cheated on us at gin, but I know better. She was just magic, that's all.

After the game of gin, she would bring out her red nail polish and begin the ritual. Each stroke had to be perfect, and after it, the brush had to be dipped in the little jar again, until there was a bead of red almost falling from it. She never slopped on a finger without afterwards removing all the polish and starting again. We were all hypnotized by the sight of it.

My favorite thing to do before I started school was to go over to her house for lunch, because every day my uncle (her son), would be there, and while she cooked for him, he would sit there and tell her how greasy her food was, and what a green-horn she was and how stupid she talked. I would say "Then why do you eat three plates of it?" or "You have great big hairs in your nose, why don't you cut them?" My mother and Bobbe would laugh, but Sherman said I had a big mouth and should be slapped, so I'd say, "Why don't you slap me? But first you'd have to catch me, and you can't run because you're too fat." I always saved the fat comment for the last, because, like all bullies, he had an achilles heel, and I knew what it was. He would always leave on the fat joke, and as he walked out, he would tell Bobbe "Maybe I'll give you a break and come by again tomorrow." I would follow him to the screen door and say, "Yeah, you'll go anywhere they got free food."

Mom and Bobbe would laugh, and then when he was gone, they would tell me that I should have respect for him, because he was my elder, and it was not ladylike to act that way to men. I would feel chastised and angry. I would feel, why can't you see that he is putting you down? You don't do anything to defend yourselves. Of course these are the words I found at a later time in my life. It is so excruciatingly painful to be a daughter, sometimes. I did not understand why you had to let people talk bad to you and not say anything back. But then, I was not yet fully indoctrinated into the ways of being a woman under Patriarchal Rule.

I think men like to pretend that they are not wholly dependent on women. Women like to pretend that they are dependent on men. And there you have it, folks, the Rosie Barr view of the BATTLE OF THE SEXES.

Bobbe also had curious and fascinating rituals with money. She would collect rent on the fifth of each month from the sixteen apartments in the building. She would then start to make the money piles. She would divide all the paper money into twenties, tens, fives, and ones. Then she would lay out the twenties first, in a cross formation, then cross that three more times with three more twenties, turning the pile into a $100.00 star formation. She would count her piles of hundred dollar stars and enter the total amount on the deposit slip then begin the same procedure with the tens, fives, and ones.

She had an extraordinary amount of coins which were divided, first into clean piles and then into dirty piles. Dirty coins were made of copper; clean coins were made of silver and predated 1950. The second division was made by denomination again, quarters, nickels, dimes, pennies. Each denomination was then housed in its own lace hankie, tied and knotted so she could reuse and recycle the clean coins, assured that they had tremendous value.

She would open the hankies every morning

after her morning prayers and count out fifteen piles of eighteen cents, eighteen being the corresponding number to the Hebrew letters in the word *chai,* meaning life. She would drop eighteen cents into a blue charity box for herself, and eighteen cents for each of her children and grandchildren (except for her daughter-in-law, the shiksa whose life she made miserable). She felt this ritual would protect and assure that we all would be protected from disease, famine, and the encroaching goyim, and insure us a long and healthy life. This ritual was called giving *tsedakah,* which means giving your fair share. Every three months, she would count all of the charity boxes (pushkas) by stacking the coins again in piles of quarters, dimes, etc. When a total count had been garnered, a check would be written in the appropriate amount and donated to Hadassah Hospital, her favorite charity. The piles of coins were further divided into clean and dirty and put back into the corresponding hankies.

Many people accuse Jews of loving money; I'm sure some readers of this page are amongst them. Let me set you straight. Jews do not love money, Jews love food and Jews love stories and Jews love life. The food and life parts are the reason we acquire money because we comprehend that those piles of quarters may buy us our lives at any given time in any given country with any given peoples who really believe that money and God are the same thing.

The story I most remember about Bobbe now, because perhaps it's the story that taught me the most in my life, happened on Friday night in her kitchen. My little brother was continually bouncing a ball on the floor and my father, not known for his tolerance or patience, kept screaming at him to stop it. What he and everyone else understood was that, while you were in Bobbe's house, the children were allowed to get away with more than at any other place on earth. She said to Daddy, "Let him bounce his ball, what does it hurt?" Father, needing to assert himself over the woman who really controlled his wife, his children and his life, said "He is my kid, I'll tell him what to do, stay out of this. Ben, stop bouncing that ball. Now." He had that tone of voice that terrified us, because violence could follow. I got an upset stomach, because I did not know what Bobbe would do then, as I had always seen every woman back down to every man, as that was the culture at the time. I knew that if Bobbe did nothing, then her magical powers and her strength would diminish in my eyes. I could understand her deferring to her son, as he was pitiful, and she always said "Just feel sorry for him."

But what could she do now? This man was her daughter's man, and he was our father. He was young and strong and she was old and fat. Half of me wanted her to shut up because he was the man, and I knew, somewhere, that women did not stand up to men, instead you let them think they were in charge. My mother had always told me that.

She did not stop; she began to shake, slightly. She said "He can bounce his ball in my house." Father was uncontrollable at that point, so insulted, so put down that he walked over and hit my little brother full force in the back of the head. Mother, ever the peacemaker, pointed her finger at my little brother, who was all of three years old and said "See? now stop!"

The tension was unbearable. Bobbe rose, like a Goddess from her red kitchen chair, hobbled over to where my father was standing, breathing hard, like he always did when he had just proved something through brute strength and she slapped him across the face with all the power of her three hundred pounds. Time froze then, and I saw all the blood drain from his face. He had a slack jaw and saucered eyes. Then she spoke "You do not hit MY grandchildren, do you understand?"

This was the first time anyone had ever stood up for us against our father. For a second he looked at her as if he would kill her. You could see his breath and his wheels churning. She said, "So now you'll beat me, too, huh?" and stood there, defiant powerful, the birth giver, bread giver, Destroyer, Nemesis.

Father, choking back sobs, said "Helen, get your coat and the kids, we're never coming back here again." He went out to the car and sat there honking the horn. Mother did not get up immediately, because Bobbe said "Let him wait." We all took our time getting on our coats and Bobbe kissed all of us, for a long, slow time. The horn stopped honking, mother was, for the first time now, standing up to her football-hero husband, and as we left, I turned to look at her kiss Bobbe good-bye, and Bobbe said "Will you be here for Shabbas?" Mother thinking for a full minute said, "Yes." That was it, it was over.

We drove home in silence and me and my sister Geraldine were elbowing each other in the back seat. We couldn't wait to get home, go to our room and impersonate Bobbe doing the "Showdown at Park Street." Sometimes, being a daughter is remarkable.

When Bobbe got sick I was already married and had three children. For many years, she had not been well, and mother thought about putting her in a rest home. But Bobbe insisted that if she ever would leave her home, it would be the thing that killed her. She tried every stop gap measure. But finally she became incontinent and the floor between her bedroom and the bathroom became stained with pee as she would try to make it to the toilet from her bed. On the last day she was at home, she fell in the pee and laid there for four hours, against a heating vent that burned the flesh of her leg. She had diabetes, and the wound would not heal. Then she knew she had to go.

She was carried from the apartments that she never left in twenty years, except for the High Holidays, trips to the doctor, and to have her hair styled at Gail Rudy's, her hairdresser.

Geraldine was able to fly from Denver back to Salt Lake. She took watermelon and bagels and her violin to Bobbe's bedside at the rest home. They ate together, and then she played "Kol Nidre" on the violin for Bobbe, because it was her favorite comforting song.

The last time I talked to her, she asked me to come home; I told her I would be able to come in five days, it would have been payday then, I would have been able to scrape together the fifty dollars to fly home. She said . . . "That's too long," and then she said goodbye. I begged her not to say goodbye, I said over and over, "please, just say goodnight, Bobbe." And for the first time in my life she told me that she loved me.

I knew then, I just knew then.

My brother told me that when he went to visit her on the last day she was ever on earth, he was walking down the hall, and he saw her naked on the bed with her red fingernail polish cracked and jagged. He covered her, and sat there holding her hand, and then she was gone.

When Bobbe died, I felt that an era had passed with her; a very very long era of exile and I wrote and read a poem over Bobbe's grave the day she was buried; I wrote it because I could find no prayer in all of Judaism to thank her (or any Jewish woman)—no way to say goodbye.

Mary Bitnam Davis 1906–1982

As Rachel and Esther
she was a Jew and a woman
A keeper of the Holy flame
the guardian of commandments
Handed down from
mothers to daughters
She kept her people from hunger
and fed them only sanctified food
She gave her life to Torah
and made all the sacrifices

She gave her husband the luxury of time
the luxury of his studies

She gave birth to us all and
      wrapped her strong arms defiantly
      around our history
Sure of her birthright
      She created Proud Men
Her strength would seize my young heart
      as I watched her create fire and pray

Her resistance; her fight with god
      her command of the only life the world
would
      allow her

In the end it was her strength that took her
      before weakness invaded
      Her tears were always betrayed

And when she felt she could resist no longer
      she rested
With Judith and Asherah.

and over her grave eleven months later:

Come to me in the exact plotted centre of the
night
When the moon spins gold waves
and they shimmer
bursting through the congealed brown of mother
      earth's belly
Arise and awake and be born
      jezebel renamed

I conjure you in the name of the daughters of the
      daughters

of the daughters
Come! with your seared flesh and toothless mouths
with torn bowels and uteruses stuffed with fetishes

And we will dance upon the earth
smelling fetid and of olives
dancing as high as flames
smoking ash rising
raining down columns of furious fire

daughters of the daughters of the daughters of
Sarah who looked into the face of god
and laughed

CHAPTER

3

Everyone is usually so very interested to know about what it was like to grow up in Salt Lake City. One really need not do more than drive through Salt Lake to appreciate its esthetic beauty. The city is a basin located at the foothills of the Wasatch Mountains, which completely encase and encircle "Happy-Valley" (as it is fondly called by its natives and happy residents). The mountains act as a natural fortress keeping "WORLDLY" (as non-Mormons are lovingly called) thoughts and visitors out and happy residents busy with new gardening projects in. In the olden days when the territory of Deseret (yet another happy name for the Beehive state) was being settled, the mountains provided not only clean sparkling water and granite rock for building but also allowed for a militaristic protection from the encroaching Federal Troops sent by Washington to control and monitor the acquisition of land and wives. So fierce was the Mormon belief in land acquisition and polygamy, they formed an army called the Mormon Militia to meet the federal troops.

The populace at that time was comprised of Saints from Illinois and some from as far away as Wales, Ireland, England, and Scandanavia. Immigrants who were newly converted to Mormonism from Europe came in search of a land flowing with milk and honey and a way to escape the potato famines. These brave frontiersmen and women were met at the boat on the shores of the Atlantic and given push carts for the long 3,000 mile journey through the mountains. With undying faith they began the trek. Those who did not die held strong to their dreams of owning land and planting and maintaining well-trimmed gardens and yards. I grew up with the descendants of these Youngs and Johnsons and Smiths.

On the corner lived the Smiths, a typical family of fourteen. The mom and dad worked very hard while gramma looked after the kids when she wasn't busy screaming at the many cats that lived in the house, sucking relentlessly on her dental plates, or watching TV. I remember watching her accidentally step on one of the new born kittens. She was a brave woman. She got the dustpan and broom and I marvelled at her courage in picking the poor thing up and disposing of it in the trash.

I remember when the brothers of the family started digging in the earth of their backyard to create a family garden. Every morning when I went over, the garden became a bigger and deeper hole. They cleverly disguised it by putting a big cardboard and tarp platelet on it, but their sister, Sherri, my best friend, and I would sneak over to it, lift it very gingerly, and look under. It was summertime so we didn't have school, and the boys could dedicate themselves to the dig. Bobby told us they were going to dig their way to China, and everyday I remember getting this mental picture of what those Chinese people would look like, as they emerged from that hole, startled, and pleasantly surprised to be in America, liberated as it were, from having to stand upside down on the earth. They would all have long robes and pointy hats like Hop Sing on "Bonanza."

While the boys kept busy digging, I was busy with Sherri playing with my first Barbie Doll. Sherri and I would stick straight pins in her boobs so it would look like she had nipples, as I was very concerned that she did not look lifelike. We loved Barbie and spent hours planning her wedding and getting her ready for a date. We would play beauty parlor with her and fix up her hair.

I used to have to get up in the morning, help my mom clean the house, and practice the piano for half an hour every day before I could join my friends who would start playing by 8:30. By 11:00 I could come out and play for an hour before Mom called me for lunch. The Smith kids could eat lunch whenever they wanted to. I was jealous too that when I would go into Sherri's house she could take a loaf of white bread and eat the center out of it. There were about seven loaves of white bread sitting on their counter, and that is what they ate for lunch everyday.

We would make Barbie doll clothes out of old discarded things around the house, socks, towels, etc. We would ride our bikes around the Safeway parking lot. We also liked to jump rope and we had our jump rope songs that we would sing, some of them we knew we could not sing around home, so we would go into the alley to do it; like, "Fudge, Fudge, tell the judge, mama had a newborn baby, wrap it up in tissue paper, send it down the elevator, first floor stop, second floor stop." "Twenty-four robbers came a knockin at my door," "Spanish dancer do the splits, spanish dancer give a high kick, Spanish dancer touch the ground, Spanish dancer turn around, Spanish dancer, get out of town."

I loved early summer because the smell of blooming gardens was everywhere and the excess mountain water was being driven down to the Jordon River (which emptied into the Great Salt Lake) via the gutters of most all neighborhood streets. Gutter day was Tuesday and all the kids cooled-off by playing barefoot in the gutters. I was never allowed to be barefoot or to join in, my mother fearing that I might become contaminated, contract polio, hookworm or worse. When I protested the injustice of not being able to participate in normal play activities, my parents broke down, purchased a pair of yellow spongey thongs for me, which allowed me the opportunity to frolic with the other children. With my new yellow thongs I was no longer limited to just my own gutters, but I was free to explore the gutters of many adjacent streets, up Belmont, to McClelland, past Eddie Hansen's where an assortment of dead and skinned animals from deer to skinned cats could be drying on the clothesline, next to the family wash, past Old Clem's, the deaf man who collected innumerable radios. I liked Old Clem and I used to buy him his radios at the corner Rexall store even though his wife Joanna forbade it. The Rexall man would always ask, "You are not buying this for Old Clem are you? His wife said that I cannot sell him anymore radios." Buying radios for Clem was such a small gesture, it seemed to make him so happy. He would get a new one, hold it in his hands, begin to dance back and forth, rocking out to the beat that he could not hear, but perhaps feel.

The water gushed deepest up on 10th East near the house where the two girls tied string from tree to tree across the sidewalk. I watched as the kid drove her bike into the string and as the paramedics began the subsequent clean up of her decapitation.

The string house was next to the McDonald house—typical neighborhood family who, like almost every Utah Mormon family, had what is called a "Special Spirit," which is a child who is retarded, crippled, or very developmentally disabled. Special Spirits are the children you can see in the front yards, picking weeds from the family gardens eight to ten hours a day while listening to transistor radios, with a happy smile upon their faces, and waiting for the mailman to happily deliver the mail that might include delivery of that special ordered gardening tool purchased from an outside catalogue.

Everyone seemed happy in "Happy Valley" except for me. Before I was able to understand that Special Spirits were the result of too much nerve gas testing and too much ancestral intermarriage among the first valley settlers, I used to pray frequently to God and ask that I might be made into a special spirit or a Mormon so that I too could enjoy my life being happy, wearing that stunned ox-like expression. Tuesdays were always happy days.

One day I went back to the Smiths to check on the hole. It was huge by now. The brothers let us climb down. I was afraid, it smelled like dead cats. There were three layers to the hole now, and one of them had a couch in it. There were pictures of naked women and cigarette butts everywhere. One day the cops came and hauled a ton of stolen toasters, radios, clocks and many other small appliances out of there. There was even a washing machine down there where cats were tortured and given baths. The cops made the boys fill in the hole, and they all got in lots of trouble.

As summer ended, gutter day stopped, and it became necessary to invent new forms of play. While many of the Utah children began to prepare for the autumnal deer hunting season, cleaning weapons and purchasing orange clothing and vests, I spent a lot of time planning parties. When all of the party guests were assembled at your house each would be given a list of items such as buttons, hair pins, pennies, and the like that you would have to return with. You went house to house throughout the neighborhood in teams, introduced yourself, told the answerer that you were on a "Scavenger Hunt" asked if they had any of the following listed items, everyone understood that there was a time limit, would invite you in while they scurried to find the item for you. The first "Team" back to my house would win the prize. Scavenger hunting for me was far more fun than I could imagine deer hunting to be for them. I didn't have to kill, skin, or gut any life form and I had the added bonus of actually going inside other homes of people like the Martins who lived two doors down.

Mrs. Martin was a bell-butted woman like a lot of Mormon women, with a bouffant hairdo. She lived with her husband, who had an assemblage of old junk cars and engine parts spewn throughout the backyard, her two overweight daughters, her slightly effeminate son, and her father in law, Old Man Martin, whose home it used to be before she took it over and banished him to a life in the upstairs attic room. They were good upstanding Mormon citizens. Mrs. Martin used to empty her postum jar and fill it with Folgers Coffee, I guess thinking that she was fooling whoever was looking, which really wasn't anybody, maybe God, but wouldn't he have known anyway?

Mrs. Martin was famous for saying "It is not up to my standards." This included me playing with her daughters, because I was often hell-bent on getting in trouble. I made Pammy do bad things according to her mother. Like the time when we put Pammy's rabbit into the washer because his feet were dirty and we broke his neck. That wasn't anything I did to get into trouble; it was out of sheer caring; the desire for purity and cleanliness which was aroused in me by living with Mormon folk. Later when I was a teenager the word got out that I smoked, that I had actually tried marijuana, which besides the inevitable coming addiction to heroin, would make me want to break into the Martin residence and steal their valuables in order to support my habit, as there was a huge underground demand for doilies and afghans on the street. Anyway, Mrs. Martin did not allow me to hang with her daughters as I was not up to her standards, which included a lot of valium consumption—still the favored drug of many Mormon women.

They were pretty broke as was everyone on our block. They sold parts from the junk cars in their backyard. When her husband took out a bank loan for his face lift it was the talk of the neighborhood. Her husband was a violent man. My Dad used to always say . . . "If a guy hunts and owns guns, what do you expect?"

Upstairs in the attic lived Old Man Martin. I guess he was suffering from Alzheimer's disease or perhaps some kind of phantom consciousness which, God knows what that would be, perhaps chemical or perhaps the remnant of a thinking person being slowly murdered by boredom in Salt Lake. One day when his family had journeyed to Murry to visit their vastly numerous family tree, he came over to our house and asked my sister Geraldine to help him paint the house with butter, which was, he said, to seal it, and so she did. She was an adventurous young girl and she was over painting the wooden house with a nice big paint brush full of melted butter. When Mother saw her and demanded that she return home, and questioned her about why she wanted to help him paint the house with butter, she remarked, "Well, because he asked me to."

Old Man Martin used to come over to our house every Thursday on garbage day. He loved my mother, as did several men around the neighborhood. He, however, was not one of the many men who loved mother who later committed suicide. He would come over every Thursday to empty our garbage and Mother always appreciated it. One time he got up, he set his alarm and it didn't work, he came running down the stairs to get our garbage, he fell down all the stairs. He came over bloody—elbows, knees, hands, face, all scraped up and Mother bandaged him and he said, "I was afraid. I was late getting your garbage off the back porch." After Mother had doctored him and he had returned home Father said, "That'll teach the old bastard to get up on time." We all had a big roar over that one.

Mr. Martin (Old man Martin's son and Mrs. Martin's husband) was an inventive, mechanical sort of guy. When he wasn't tinkering on his old cars, he was inventing new techniques to rid the neighborhood of the excessive cat population. He would catch them, trap them in pillowcases and tie the pillowcases to the exhaust pipes of his many old cars and gas them. He was often seen emptying pillowcases into the huge trash barrels out back in the alley.

On scavenger hunts I would always ask Mrs. Martin for empty coffee cans. She never had any.

You could usually count on getting an empty coffee can from our next-door neighbors, the Kings. There was the wife Heather, another obese woman, her husband Dick, who might have weighed 110 pounds. He was a self-proclaimed weekend alcoholic. He worked in a candy store, he always brought home candy for his wife and three children. I used to babysit for them, I liked to go over there because as soon as they were gone I could go into his closet with his piles and piles of nudist magazines and see all kinds of slightly ugly people playing volleyball in the sun, and then of course, seems like over the years, the nudity and the magazines increased, including all the men's magazines like *Hustler* and whatever. I did love to babysit them to look at the nude portraits.

Their house was very close to ours and you

could hear everything that went on there. I remember one summer night when the cats outside the window were moaning in heat. They sounded like babies crying. The cat calls went on for hours. It must have been a weekend because Mr. King was very drunk. He boiled a pot of water and when he opened the door to throw the water on the cats, he tripped and scalded his legs. He was burned quite badly and was out of work for a while. During this time he used to come to our house often and ask to borrow a glass of ice. You would fill the glass up and he would thank you and go across the street to the Athertons's house.

The Athertons were the only Catholics on the block. He would ask them to fill the glass with alcohol. They usually obliged. The father of the Athertons was the most respected man on the block. They had the nicest house. They were intelligent people. Mr. Atherton was a research scientist at the University of Utah. I later found out that he was working on a cure for cancer, experimenting on many cats in his laboratory.

CHAPTER

4

We lived on Park Street, in Salt Lake, in a big tenement slum which my grandparents owned. After WW II, they sponsored several Jewish survivors from Nazi-ville, and almost every one of the twelve apartments were filled at one time by these people. My parents and I lived in one apartment under Leo the Basque Sailor, who never left his apartment, like my grandmother, and so they had it worked out with the grocery store to just bring them weekly food, which they would pay for. My grandmother devised this plan, because she was an elitist, like most Jewish people from Lithuania were, and she would say "I do not SHOP," like it was a foul ritual of the lower classes. My grandmother was of the lower classes too, but she was Queen of our family, and we all believed that Queens and Commoners don't mix.

In our family, the first born daughter succeeds to the throne after the oldest Crone dies (*Crone* meaning wise woman). My mother now holds this position, and when she dies, it will be me.

Robbie the babysitter lived on one side of us, and on the other side lived my mom's brother, Hymie, slob extraordinaire, his wife and their eventual child Jeff, aged two. Above and over lived Mr. and Mrs. Rosenberg, both survivors of Auschwitz, and their American-born child, Boobyline.

Every Friday night for Shabbas, the entire clan

would congregate in Bobbe's apartment for dinner, dancing and the telling of the stories, which were about how ten years previous, one-third of all the people who looked like us were disappeared from the earth.

There was a big window sill where I created the Las Vegas–style entertainment that came almost mystically to me back then at the age of three. All the family loved my act and used to call me "Sarah Bernhardt." The stage was the only place in Utah where I felt safe. I entertained like mad, because I was afraid if I didn't everyone would start to talk about the Holocaust, while I longed for my childhood (which I found at age twenty-eight). When it would happen anyway, I tried to go into the bedroom and put pillows over my ears, or watch TV with the sound up loud, or sing to myself. Still, I always heard and I was afraid. I didn't understand geography, I thought that these horrible things had happened just down the street, on the next block, very close to me. Now I feel it was even closer than that. It was one breath away.

One particular Friday night, I locked myself in the bathroom and proceeded to levitate around the room, there was a very high window, and rising up to it I saw, sailing through the air, a man on a horse who looked like my grandfather, Ben, who had died a few years before. He was waving at me and telling me to hang on, that I would be alright, that he would see to it that God wouldn't take any more little Jewish girls right now, because He still had Anne Frank. This is the story I see in every Marc Chagall painting.

Sometimes, still, I feel like I could weep, just lay my head in my hands, and let go with some great flood that would drown the world. I am always at the edge of collapse, in this world when I think about how fragile everything is, and how we, like spiders and ants and bees spend our lives trying to create safety, a web, a hill, a hive, and yet there is no such thing, and realizing this, I will, for a while, feel great hollow awe.

There were no other Jews in our neighborhood. I was always the only Jew at my school, and so very paranoid. I always felt the onslaught of the Nazis was very close. When we played Barbies, I said why do we always have to play like she's getting ready for a wedding or a date, why don't we do some thing daring? Like say she's a resistance fighter parachuting behind enemy lines with a secret code to save people? The Mormon girls would say "Oh, I'm sure, Roseanne. You have to be her cousin Skipper."

The most important thing for a girl in Utah was to prepare herself for marriage, so, in school, we all took Home Ecch. The teacher: "Home Economics prepares you for life as it really is, girls. This semester we'll be learning to bake a one-egg cake, make a colorful housecoat, and crochet a map of the known universe." Me: "Well, how about if we learned to crochet, say, some secret message or code into a scarf—like Madame Defarge in *Tale of Two Cities?* Like, if we're ever resistance fighters parachuting behind enemy lines, to, like you know, save some people?"

"No, Roseanne, we're gonna learn cross stitching." At school, I felt like I was always the "designated Heathen," especially at Christmas time where all of us would sing the sacred songs of a foreign God and Religion. Now I'm actually very pleased about it . . . about being Other. But anyway, at the Christmas pageants I was the designated Heathen and would first sing the little song about the Dreidl, and then tell about why Jews don't believe in Jesus . . . a very nice and civil way of excluding me by "including." And so very democratic, as I was always reminded by the good open-minded teachers in Utah that had we been in a Communist country, I would never have been allowed to express my religion, because "dissent" is not tolerated there. Oh, my religion was a religion of dissent, strange, exotic and somehow always threatening. This made me a bad person, and somehow, I knew it. My little Dreidl song went something like this . . . "Dreidl, dreidl, dreidl, I made it out of clay, it contains a secret code for partisan fighters parachuting behind enemy lines today."

They never understood our Holidays, either. When we would have Passover, I would have lurid fantasies about them seeing us, and telling each other about it. When we would have fun hiding the matzo, and then the youngest child finds and brings it to your grandpa, as a ransom, the child can ask for any amount of money, and the service cannot continue until the ransom is paid. I could imagine them telling their parents, or other people . . . "Well, the grandpa hides the crackers and then the youngest Jew makes him pay money, or they can't eat. It's like the magic bread or something, everyone drinks wine, even the kids, and then they fill a glass and open the door to let in a spirit of a dead guy who drinks the wine too. . . . They sing songs in a foreign language, it's just gotta be some sort of a secret code. . . . ''

There was only one safe place on earth to be Jewish then, one safe place against the imagined and real onslaught of terrorism, and that was at my Grandma's house, at her oil cloth–covered kitchen table, where she, as Resistance fighter, listened constantly to the talk radio show, and when there was anything anti-Semitic in the conversation (i.e., everyday) she would call in, and using a secret code (wisdom, truth) set them straight.

When I was a little girl growing up in Salt Lake City, we could say anything we wanted to in our home as long as it was funny. We could never express ourselves out and out, but since we were Jewish there was always glorious food for sublimating feelings. And anyway, what did expression matter, as we were in Utah, where the expressions of religious awe and anti-communist disdain were all that counted anyway.

Helen and Jerry who are to this day my parents were delightful and deeply in love with their respective mothers, as well as each other. When Daddy was in a good mood (which was extremely rare) he would do fun things with us children like hide and squirt us with the hose, dance around in his underwear, or lift a leg and let loose with a creature release. Mother would say, "Now Jerry, your children are young ladies and gentlemen, set a good example for them," and then he would say OK and grab his huge beer gut and belch at her.

Sometimes Mother would get mad, and not talk to Daddy, and sometimes she would laugh and sometimes she would cry . . . whatever she would do, he would always apologize to her and then they would kiss in that grotesque manner which only one's parents can do (and turn a young girl's developing heart, mind, and stomach into a huge black void). Their displays of parent-passion were enough to psychically cripple all four of their children forever, sending me in particular into a state of sexual paralysis, with dreams of worms and fish, until many years later, when I was aroused for the first time by the man I later married (and made a fortune making fun of).

When I first met my husband in 1971, he was reading a copy of *The Sensuous Man*, he had very long hair and leather moccasins—every hippie woman's dream. At the time I had left home (like all Jewish girls) in order to eat pork and take birth control pills.

When I first shared an intimate evening with my husband, I was swept away by the passion (so dormant inside myself) of a long and tortured existence. The physical cravings I had tried so hard to deny, finally and ultimately sated. . . . But enough about the pork.

CHAPTER 5

Two widow sisters sold the house to Mom and Dad for ten thousand dollars which Bobbe paid cash for. I was always intrigued about widows and sisters living together and I have already made plans with my sister Geraldine that if we are ever widowed we must live together in a house with several cats, although I don't like cats but it seems to go together.

The house had wood floors and we'd always get slivers in our feet because we couldn't afford to buy a new rug. Daddy would paint and varnish whenever we kids were getting too many slivers. We turned the attic into my room; I had a white carpet and I painted the walls orange, and then I wrote quotes from the Book of Deuteronomy in Hebrew all over my door and the walls in orange, with peace signs later on in the sixties—heralding the doom of all mankind. You could open the doors and go out on the roof and smoke. Mother would never catch me smoking, I thought, but as soon as we would go to school, Mother would be going through our drawers and our diaries, as was advised by the Mormon leaders, to make sure that we weren't on drugs. Unfortunately for me, when I was sixteen, I did have marijuana in my room so I never heard the end of that. And I took to writing fantasies of a sexual nature in my diary which Mother took as God's honest truth. Though I was a virgin who'd never been kissed, Mother was sure that I was a slut; I remember one story I wrote about being in bed with ten men and of course Mother believed it.

When we figured her snooping out, we removed the doorknobs from our rooms and hid them under our beds because you couldn't get into our rooms without the doorknob. Sometimes we would be locked in our room and scream for each other—"I need that *doorknob*"—and someone would go out, search around and invariably find it and let you out of your room. But we didn't have much privacy and later we learned how to open the doors with knives, so the silverware from the kitchen would be minus any knives and they would all be up in our rooms somewhere along with little cigarette butts and roaches.

I loved our basement. It was all cinder blocks and spider webs and you'd go down several stairs and you'd have to feel with your hands to find the light which you never exactly knew where it was and sometimes if you made the mistake of touching the bulb and not the string you'd get a little shock. But while we would go down there searching for the light we would have to close our eyes because there were hangers on clotheslines and we were always afraid, particularly my little sister Geraldine, having nightmares of getting hangers in the eyes and the nose.

This is the basement that I remember with that cold terror that you get when you watch a horror movie, and it's always in a dark dungeon that's exactly like the first basement you ever saw.

I believe that basements can only scare you

once, the first time you see them, and after that, you can witness any basement and be OK about knowing that basements do exist. But this first basement is the basement I return to over and over again in my mind. For instance, this is the basement where the guy from *Psycho*'s mother was, and it was also here that the various mad scientists cooked up their evil chemicals to poison the world, and where escaped psychos hid out and of course, where monsters and such can dematerialize and hibernate, invisibly, until some poor fat little girl comes down there to retrieve something for her mother. A child had to retrieve the jar of peaches or such, while her mother stood at the top of the stairs with the door wide open so she could answer when her daughter cried "Mama, are you still standing there?" "Yes, Roseanne, I'm still standing here. You're meshugga, do you know that?" "Yes Mother. Why don't you just come down here yourself?"

"I don't like it down there either," Mother would call.

As a teenager, I would go down there to sneak cigarettes behind the big boiler and write the word *fuck.* I was always enchanted with the word *fuck,* I still am. It's my favorite word. It's the only word that is a verb and noun and adverb and everything else. It's beautiful and coarse and ugly all at the same time. And it's excruciatingly shocking, so of course I had to write it. People say, well, only uneducated people swear, and I must say au contraire— only the educated prefer to remove any kind of colorful language from their speaking patterns 'cause they're brain dead, or as my father says "they have that well-scrubbed look, like they reached in their brain and scrubbed it all out." That's how father used to describe Mormons. Or the educated, or the non-Jew, or whoever he happened to be speaking of at the time.

Next door to us lived the Chacons: Rosie, Ester, Bobbie, Cece, Darlene, Rudy and Ronnie, and the mom, YaYa, and the dad Roberto, and they used to open their windows and yell to us we killed their God.

Daddy always had a joke or two about boobs. We would go around and around and he would say things about women and I would say things about him and we would have contests and showdowns and I would always win. My father taught me that comedy is mightier that the sword and the pen. And even though he was a sexist pig, if I would say something that was very anti-male, or anti-him, and it was funny, my father would applaud and say "good one."

Every summer we would put on the proverbial neighborhood play. Sherri and I would spend a few days writing it, and it always had music, we would sing the popular songs of the day with a few word changes that approached parody (at least in the eleven-year-old mind). We would force all of our friends and our little sisters Chris and Geraldine into playing the foils. We would work and cut costumes out of construction paper, drag the record player and the Beach Boys records out to the garage, practice for a few days and then print up tickets and invitations.

Mostly it would just be our parents and siblings who came, but my mom, whom we called Miss Hattie, would be sure every time to call up all her friends who didn't live around us, and they would come over too. All the parents would applaud nicely, except my parents: Miss Hattie would always cheer just a bit too much, and so would my daddy. I could always be assured of their standing ovation for all my efforts. Sometimes Daddy would bring home men that he worked with. My mom and dad would always go out of their way for me and my plays, Mom would make her famous punch or cookies or jello for refreshments, and even my piano lessons and other assorted important things could be put on hold when I was engaged in writing.

One of Daddy's friends who popped his gum and smelled like Old Spice, Mr. Fowler, always talked about his gun collection and insurance. In fact, he came to our home to sell insurance to us and, like so many people, decided to stay, becoming a devotee of the Barr family, as Mom and Dad were quite amusing and took great pains to be and remain so.

So it was quite disappointing when we heard one day that he had gone into his gun room, and swallowed the barrel. Of course Daddy had the best jokes about it, that Mr. Fowler had spent an evening with our family and blown his brains out. It seemed a common occurrence that year. Mother's handyman George was working for her and one afternoon he took off early. We were quite disheartened when we heard that he had that afternoon gone to his home for lunch, and then hung himself in his front room. The next day us children ran up the street to try to peer into the window to see him hanging there, but he had already been chopped down.

We lived on Lincoln Street, a street with a lot of noise on it because there were a lot of kids who lived there. It was a street where kids would hang out, because hardly any cars would ever come down and if one did, you would know the person in it. It was a street where a car would come every day at 5:25, and so when you were standing in it, at 5:22, you would know, all of you, that you had to move in approximately three minutes. It was a street where you would know not to be on at all on Friday nights, because Mr. Darling would be coming home drunk and would plow into you, or into the Stop sign at the corner which he ran down every few years. You never talked to his daughter Utahna about her dad's drunkenness, you all just ignored it because she was your friend, and it was not that odd because that was the kind of a street it was.

It was also the kind of street where a girl could go door to door and ask "Do you have any chores I could do for pay?" and your friend Sherri Ann Smith's part would come next. "We need $25 each to go to camp this summer." Every person in every house would give you a chore and pay you each 50 cents. I would borrow the last $10 from Bobbe, and Sherri from her grandma, and we would go to camp every summer. It was the kind of street where Mr. and Mrs. Strong would let you come over and look at their backyard where they had placed 150 elves, deer, trolls, flamingos, and a stone wishing well and a tool shed that looked like a gingerbread house. They would give you ice water and ask you if you were doing good in school. They had sixty-four grandchildren, but loved all of us kids too.

Not long after we moved into the eighty-year-old Lincoln St. house, Mama started nagging Daddy to fix up the place and make it more inhabitable. It was inhabitable, but Mother had an urge to redecorate because it was the first house she ever owned.

We found the the prior tenants—old widows—had been quite the decorators themselves. Each wall had about seventy-five layers of wallpaper. Mama wanted Daddy to paint, but the paint wouldn't stick to the wallpaper, so Daddy got a spatula and tried to peel it off but it wouldn't come off, so then he got a sponge and he tried to make it wet but that didn't work, so he went out in the yard and brought in the hose and squirted all the walls and proceeded to try to scrape it off again, and chunks of wallpaper and wall started to slowly detach. Piles and piles of wallpaper and wall grew in the middle of the room. This took weeks, and Mama was starting to get mad. She told him that this was going to take too long.

Then Daddy got the idea to go to Howie Rents. He brought home a wallpaper-eating machine with a huge nozzle thing and a generator fueled by kerosene. For about ninety days, this machine just started to really eat wallpaper and the piles were getting so huge that when you came home from school you had to throw the full weight of your body against the front door, just to scrape the wallpaper out of the way so that you could get in. Then you would have to walk all over wet wallpaper that smelled like kerosene. Daddy finally got down to the bare walls, but by then they had been destroyed, and Mother had to hire a carpenter to come in and build all new ones. Carpenter #1 was driving home one day and a big beam of steel came up from the back of his truck and pierced his body. Luckily, he did not die, but he did stay a very long time in the hospital.

The house's wiring was very old and when Mama would mop over an outlet on the floor, fires would spring up—but only little fires. Until one day when a great big fire started in the basement. The firemen came and yelled at Mom and Dad about having bad wiring, a house full of kerosene-soaked paper and four children.

Mom and Dad then painted the old bricks on the outside of the house a nice bright green, including the front steps which were cement. Then they hired another carpenter to come and sandblast it off. Carpenter #2 later killed himself.

There was no separation between my brother's room and the girls' room, so Daddy stapled a sheet into the wall so we couldn't see each other, but could whisper at night and hear perfectly well. Mom and Dad let us kids deface the hallway wall with graffiti and pictures, which we proudly showed off to our friends, who would think we had the coolest parents in the world.

My Bobbe Fanny, Daddy's mom, decorated our house in little knickknacks that she would sell at fairs and craft shows. There were little chairs made out of old beer cans, and dolls' heads that held potholders, and dolls' heads that held extra toilet paper, and dolls' heads attached to a doll's dress that covered toasters and blenders. There were rocking chairs made out of wooden clothes-pins, and yarn covers for coke bottles that had dog-gie heads, and yarn triangles with a wire through them that you could bend and find a Hershey's Kiss.

My favorite story was when Mother had de-cided that it was time to build a music room in the unfinished basement (which had an assortment of rat-catching devices, carcasses of dead rats and mice, and ivy growing through the cracks in the brick stones). She answered an ad in the Salt Lake *Tribune* that merely said, "We Haul Everything." Four large men from the island of Tonga appeared at the door. Mother directed them to the piano, a gift given her by her father when she was a profi-cient teenage pianist. The men were told to "Haul the piano out through the kitchen door and down the basement steps." There were four steps down and then, at a right angle, four more steps. At the bottom of these steps was the pantry area of the basement where mother, like all good, concerned Utahans, kept her twelve-year-old jars of peaches.

Two men stood in the front of the upright piano, two men stood behind it. As they started to carry it down the first four steps they broke off all the banisters, dropped the piano on its side and left it balanced on the landing. The two men that were carrying the rear of the piano were trapped in the basement. They found and opened many of the jars of peaches while the other two partners left to get what they called a hydraulic jack to "Jack off the last four remaining stairs leading to the basement."

By the time they returned the beginning stages of botulism had set in with the fourth partner. They squoze him through the doorway and the piano by lifting it straight in the air and then dropping it, which ruined the piano and its ornately carved wooden case. The fourth partner was in the back yard vomiting profusely when the other three men hauled him away, leaving the piano on its side, the balcony and banisters destroyed. My father was expected home from his job at Sears at 5:00. It was now 2:30.

My mother regained her composure and started to come up with a plan. The first thing she did was start to make the broth for barley soup; Daddy felt that barley soup was just about the best, most special thing he could eat. She then bathed and applied quite a bit of mascara that day. Mother instructed us: I was to meet Dad as the car pulled up and not let him enter the house in the usual manner through the backdoor. Instead I should give him a big hug and lead him into the kitchen and get him to sit down at the table. My sister was told to bring him his paper and we were all told to try extra hard to be nice to him and to keep the secret about what was waiting lodged in the basement. Mother met me and Dad in the kitchen and kissed him and served him his favorite meal of barley soup while we all stared at him and watched him eat it. About five minutes into this Preferred Customer treatment, Daddy stood up in a great Jackie Gleason–like movement and screamed "All Right, God Damn It, What Is Going On Here!"

Running out the back door, Daddy caught sight of the horrible remains of a staircase with a piano wedged into it. In his perfect deadpan (which I believe all of us kids inherited), he took a deep breath and remarked, "Oh, I see you moved the piano."

After sizing up the situation Daddy called his brother-in-law and two other men to come to the house. He had purchased a heavy duty pulley with a chain. They drilled into the beam of the porch roof, attached one end of the pulley to it. Using chains and rope they hoisted the piano up in the air and then swung it onto the floor of the back-porch where it still sits today—sixteen years later.

My parents were not like other kids' parents in the fifties and sixties, my dad didn't even own one jacket with patches on the sleeves and he never went around on Saturdays in dungarees. He wasn't exactly a clothes horse. He wore the same outfit for about two weeks, I guess. He was a slob. About every two weeks he'd call us kids together and say, "Kids, go draw me a bath." We'd cheer and run around, kiss our mother, clean our rooms. We'd get the bath ready and he'd go in there. We'd hear a big loud wet plop. We'd stand outside in the hall and yell, "Daddy, get under your arms, too! Daddy, don't forget to wash your hair!" We'd peek through the keyhole to make sure he was actually in the tub. Sometimes, he'd fool us though, and when we'd look through the keyhole, there would be a big pair of eyes staring back at us, or worse. Daddy was never ever ashamed of the functions of the body, except for sex, of course. Maybe in houses where the parents are not ashamed of sex they do not proudly exhibit the other (more disgusting) body functions, which the ashamed parents do as a way to compensate . . . hmmmm. . . .

My mother was different, too. When I was a little girl, there was this mean boy who called me fatso all the time. He picked on all the kids and had us all very scared. My mother told me once to go and invite him over for a piece of cake, she said she'd teach him about being nice, so I did. My mother was always a bit frightening, the way a good mother should be. She said, from inside the house, "Curtis, would you like some nice chocolate cake? Wait on the porch a minute, OK?" She had already smeared this purple facial mask on her face, and as it dried, it drew her face taut, making her eyes look very bloodshot and her lips very swollen. She took out her false teeth, and smeared ketchup all over her hands and mouth and neck. She ratted her hair way out too, and she came out, holding a piece of cake covered with about one and one-half bottles of ketchup. "Here, Curtis," she said, real slow, "here's your cake."

I'll never forget that kid's face. It turned completely white and he stood there not even breathing. "Don't pick on the other kids anymore, OK, Curtis?" she said. He just nodded. I have no doubt that mother has changed not only Curtis, but Curtis's seed, down to the fourth generation.

My mother grew up in SLC during WW II . . . so who knows how much better she might have fared psychologically had she had the good fortune to have grown up in Poland during WW II. Her hobbies were being a credit to her race and hiding in the basement. Once I remember someone knocking at the front door and my mother saying "c'mon kids," and we'd just get up and go down in the basement for about two hours, huddling there on the dark stairs. Then she would open the door and we would all come up again and resume being normal.

I used to like to scare other kids on our walks home. Once it was at night and we'd just been to church and heard a dog barking a very bizarre kind of a bark, kind of long and growly, and I convinced all the other girls that was Satan and he was after us. Everyone was screaming and hysterical, and we came over to my house and there we performed the ritual—which I was making up as I went along—to rid ourselves of the Satanic dog. And all the girls always believed that I had some kind of connection with witchy things. Mormon people are very easy to convince, because they see Satan everywhere; as I know now, Satan for them is a euphemism for "thought." Of course, I was always called to drive Satan back—I said, "Satan, get thee behind me." Everyone was quite grateful. I didn't know exactly what mysticism was then—about women. Because every first Sunday of every month was testimony meeting, where everyone stood up to "bear testimony" and the stories often included tales of being heated, being exorcised, or having God talk to you in person. It was not considered odd, but everyday, like the Pentacostals, so therefore it's not all that weird that the most important thing in the world to me has always been spirituality.

I knew always that there was really something

about women because of the witches on Halloween. They were always women, and very unattrac-
tive I might add, riding around on their brooms in
the full moon, the spinny moon as Dylan Thomas
says. And they had covens, each having always thirteen witches, which is how thirteen became an "un-
lucky" number. Anyway, I did feel some kind of
connection to some kind of other forces, and I
never let go of it.

I used to go over to our Junior High across
the street and bribe the Mexican man who was the
grounds-keeper and he would turn on the sprinklers and me and my girlfriend Sherri would roll
up our pants and take off our shoes and run from
one end of the field to the other. Or sometimes
we'd go over there and roll down the hills, try to
break into the school, write graffiti or sneak cigarettes. I loved that. There was something so wonderful about writing graffiti to deface something
that belonged to the state. I had such a criminal
mind. And sometimes I would take my notebook
over there and sit under a tree and I would pretend
that I was in Scotland or Ireland somewhere, in
great grassy green fields with my notebook like a
great drunken Irish poet.

I would walk around a few times and try to get
lost. We always like to go and get lost, down alley-
ways and rows after rows of houses and trees and
it's just like a wonderland. To go two blocks away
from home was wonderful, because you didn't really know where you were.

I always tried to walk home from school a different way and there were a lot of ways because
there were so many alleys and so many streets all

very small and all interconnected. I would imagine that there was a maniac after me, which mother encouraged. She'd say, "Well, where are you going?" "Well, we're going down to 9th and 6th." "Well, be careful, 'cause there's a murderer loose and he lived right around there." "We're going to 11th East and 13th South." "Well, be careful because there is a murderer up there." At eight o'clock you had to be in the house because you could be murdered by many things imagined, things just lurking around looking for little girls. Especially, maybe, little girls who were Jewish.

Dancing lessons cost a dollar a week and were Tuesday nights. We would be doing our tap dance, "no can do," and such, and I had such a great time with dancing lessons. There was a big glass window where I would turn and there were Sherri's brothers laughing, saying "look at fatty, look at fatty try to dance." And then Mother came one Tuesday and made me leave and I looked at her and said what's the matter. Mother was crying and said, "We can't afford a dollar a week. You can't take dancing lessons anymore." I was very brave and I said, "Well, that's okay, Sherri can teach me what she learns," and she would. She would teach me everything she learned in dance class. And I wanted to be a tap dancer, because then, I thought, well I can go into show business if I know how to tap dance, because I knew I belonged on the tube.

The AG grocery had a nice butcher who would always make jokes with the kids. We had fun going with Mom. We had bandanas and cap guns and we would run in, scream "This is a stick-up!," shoot our guns and run out. Mom had all four doors open. She drove the getaway car. We would jump in the car and drive to the park to enjoy the picnic lunch she had packed in the trunk of the getaway car. During the picnic Mom made it clear that we were not allowed to be robbers unless she was with us.

I did my first shoplifting there, at sixteen; I stole a can of baby food and was caught. I had to bring back twelve cents and apologize, and he never looked at me nicely again. I loved that baby food. Later, when I had my own children, I ate it constantly, and I still love it.

I don't think I'd love it now that I've had champagne and caviar, my favorite things to eat. I told my sister when we were in New Orleans on tour with Julio Iglesias, "you've got to taste this," and I took her to the Royal Sonesta, in a beautiful suite they had a beautiful restaurant underneath. All dressed up in black silk, I went down and told my sister, putting some on her toast point, "Before you eat this I want you to imagine we are in Russia, and we are Bolsheviks. We have just stormed the Czar's palace and we have found a jar of this and we know that this is what the Czar's been eating at the same time that we've existed on potatoes, and we open it and we put it in our mouth and it's exquisite." And my sister ate it and said, "Fish ovum, not my favorite."

Now she's a vegetarian which is probably the way to go. She could never eat meat, because when she was a little girl at age four, we went and got a turkey for Passover and she had to ride in the backseat of the station wagon with a live turkey in a cage and then we went to Bobbe's and the rabbi came over and he slit its throat and said a prayer on it in the backyard to Kosher it, and my brother could never eat chicken either; he could only eat hamburger and pizza. And every night at dinner was a battle. He would sit at one end of the table and Daddy would sit at the other end and Daddy would say eat your chicken and my brother would say, "I can't." My father would say, "You are going to sit there until you eat your chicken." My brother would start crying and say, "It'll make me vomit, I hate it." My father would say, "You are going to eat every bit of that chicken." My brother would sit, humiliated with his head down crying and Father wouldn't leave the table and sometimes it would be three hours with my father screaming at my brother to eat his chicken and berating him with "What's wrong with you?" Sometimes he would eat it and then he would run into the bathroom and throw up. He said, I hate soft meat, I can't eat soft meat. My father was determined to turn my brother into some sort of his idea of a man, and that included *a man who eats chicken!*

CHAPTER 6

I was a particularly loving little child—everyone in our neighborhood called me "Bossy." I always insisted on being the teacher when we played school, the mother when we played house, and the star of every neighborhood play. I didn't feel then (or now) that hogging all the glory is a disservice. I can do it better than anyone and, being a perfectionist, I always make sure to do everything *myself.*

Not that I believe I am without fault. I know my flesh is weak but I don't feel (as one alcoholic friend suggested) that I am displaying "alcoholic behavior" or covering up some deep seated insecurity with delusions of grandeur. I am merely *amazed* by the workings of my paranormal intelligence and the overpoweringly incredible shadings of my personality.

What's wrong with loving yourself as I do? Just because I refuse to be like most women and attempt to believe by running to seminars or shrinks that there is something foul and untrustworthy about my character. People might make the mistake of thinking that I love only myself to the exclusion of everyone else (and of course that is true), but I also love to be generous, especially with my advice—and less frequently with money. I love my family and my friends and I do whatever I can do for them, even though they selfishly insist on living their own lives, and I allow them to do that, because we all have a choice to make in this world.

I know I have a job to do while I am on this planet in this incarnation: To attempt to break every social norm, turn it back on itself and see that it is laughed at. This is the most fun thing there is on earth. I chuckle with glee if I know I have offended someone, because the people I intend to insult offend me horribly. I cannot bear the imagination of people my age at this point. I'm calling us the "What Me Worry? Generation," because Alfred E. Newman all grown up is our hero and our symbol. He didn't get any smarter, he just got power and money: Ronald Reagan, George Bush, Michael Dukakis, Jesse Jackson, Geraldine Ferraro and everyone else in power—all Alfred E Newmans.

They're leaders of a generation who have been given too much information, and cannot handle it all. Who have been told about things like world economies, and know that war is a money-making expedition, who know there never has been a weapon that hasn't been used, who know that governments cause starvation, that everything is poisoned, that we are truly, truly de-evolving . . . but just continue to refuse to know, shrug it off, and jog a lot, play squash and watch TV. Too much information did not make us evolve, it did not make us informed, it just made us want to watch "Police Academy 5," blame the victim, and masturbate a lot. We don't have the slightest clue about how to talk to each other, or what culture is even about (let alone be smart enough anymore to create it) but like a bad little three-year-old we do know how to take it apart and break it like an old toy and leave it around for mommy to clean up. I for one know that our Mommy is getting very very pissed off at us, hearing of her children begging for ridiculous things, and if I were Her what would really piss me off the worst is that they cannot even get My gender right for Christsakes.

When I was three or four, I fell on the leg of the kitchen dinette and my face froze in a manner that resembled an older person who had had a stroke. When it did not return to normal the next day, mother called the rabbi, who said a prayer for me, and nothing happened. The next day, in escalating panic, mother called the Mormon priests, because she feared that my face would mar my chances of acquiring a meal ticket at a later age. Anyway, the day after the Mormons prayed, I was miraculously "healed."

Why, you may ask (as I did at a later age), was a doctor or a health professional not contacted? Well the only rational answer to that is that we lived in Utah, where all illness, disease and mild upset is assessed to be a SIGN.

Even though we were not Mormon but Jewish, the mystique of the "new Zion" had also enveloped us and mother feared the wrath of the god of the gentiles.

When my face became healed, mother (never having lived anywhere on earth but Salt Lake City) accepted it as a sign from god that the Mormon faith was the one true religion on the face of the earth, and that she and I should join it.

But she was afraid of the wrath of her *own*

mother, and so there was a compromise. Friday, Saturday, and Sunday morning I was a Jew; Sunday afternoon, Tuesday afternoon, and Wednesday afternoon we were Mormons. So, after I learned about my people being murdered in every country but America, I could then learn about my new forbears being persecuted in Illinois, New York, and Utah. This made for a complete and well-rounded feeling of paranoia.

At the church's behest, mother travelled all over the holy city of salt proclaiming and testifying to the miracle that the Mormon priest had visited upon her daughter . . . Mother was a great public speaker, and in a way a good PR person for Jews everywhere, as those Mormons could see with their own two eyes that Mother did not possess horns, or humps, or a hammer and sickle, or the numbers 666 embedded on her forehead. In fact nothing was odd about Mother, other than the dark hair and eyes and skin, which I'm sure was frightening anyway to those fine Mormon folk, to whom Jell-O and cheese whiz are mouth-watering delights.

Then when I was about eight, Mother stayed home and I began to speak in the Mormon church. I would always give the speeches for the youth, and then later for the adults, saying "I thank God for helping my mother to find the true church, and even though all of my ancestors were murdered recently, I still know that this is the true religion of God on earth."

I was the darling of the Mormon hour, as everyone was just so very excited by the "blessing of a member of the House of Judah not going to have to spend all of eternity in hell." I was quite pleased about it myself, feeling extremely superior to those other "lost" people of Jewish, Catholic, Protestant, Buddhist, Islamic, Moslem, socialist, and Sikh belief systems who were all, unfortunately and most certainly, doomed.

I still "loved" them, though, that's what we were taught, to have Christian charity in our hearts, and still love the sinners, as they were going to be very lost for a very, very long time . . . and we did love them, unless there was a chance that they would acquire any political clout or power, thus making them enemies of our God.

I was very useful and also very popular in this very small circle, I was President of the Youth Group, and I also led the choir. People would say, "Look at our little Jeweeeesh girl, not even a member, really, and what an example she is to our own young people." I also considered it my duty to notify parents, and other authority figures if I feared that any of the other young people had strayed or sinned . . . that is how we helped each other. I remember one boy I fancied quite a bit, Eddie, who was very cute, and had very cute hair. I told him that I felt he was smoking pot, I had heard the rumor, and I was going to get "help" for him from his mother and father . . . he called me a bitch, but I forgave him, of course.

I remember at the age of sixteen I was at school, skimming through a medical journal, another of my "hobbies." Miraculously, the book just opened to the page on Bell's Palsy, which was the name of the disease which had led me into what turned out to be ten years of Mormon lifestyle. The information in the journal stated that Bell's Palsy was a temporary paralysis, usually lasting only forty-eight hours.

I only remember that I went just a wee bit mad, and started laughing and screaming at the same time. That very afternoon, I drank beer, smoked two cigarettes, tried to purchase drugs, and begged Eddie to go with me down a ravine and fuck my brains out. As a member of the church, he declined, in a manner rather like blind panic, probably thinking that I was possessed by Satan himself . . . then later that evening, he called me at home, to inquire about if I was OK, and could we still do it . . . I told him, as I have told them all . . . "Honey, you never gets a second chance."

CHAPTER

7

Letters (Age Twelve and Fifteen)

Dear Family,
        am having sooo
much fun HAHA
        I cannot stand the
stinking, puking or rotton
food. No one in our unit
likes us, but Janet Berrey.
        You know Phoebe, that
fat girl I know.
                Us three have our
own seperate tables coz we
are such slobs!
        Its fun with Janet

Tonight is Tues, I
could not write yesterday
coz of the stinking counselor
what a babe

Tell Beany I made her
an elephant for her
birthday. It has her name
on it — get the hint?

Well, have to go to a
stinking volleyball game

BART

man, dis is

SOOOO

fun

in dis jail

Write to me ::

Roseanne (TheGreat) B

arr

care of Annie,
unit 9
Brighton

for dinner we had
porcupine!! Really!!..
after recovering,
we had a rotty Indian
thing we laughed sooo
hard and it was sposed to
be serious!!   Bye, dolls
Rosie

❦

Dear Pwsweawna: (Pedersens)

As you can tell, I am taking type in school this year... 15 whole words a minut

How neat . Sherri can do 35, but as you can see, she is having more trouble than

me.

Seminary is a vkast (blast) whew, I got the highest grade on the test..I

didn't miss none!

I as going to get my guitar in five minutes..my birthday present.

Is Jeddie's birthday the 6th? If so I will make him a rag doll out of rags of

course. I got a citizenship mark out og foods, and out of science, I as doing re

really good, huh?

Eddy is a real freak-out and he makes me sick . It is a dance tonight in mutus and I'm not going becaouse (sic)----I saw that in a magazine it means mistake in spelling) of that big goggle eyed-sows ear. Boy ,do I ever hate him88888

Guess what else? I am having a blast out here.I went to see ''to sir with love'' with Cindy Atherton and we al most got thrown out because of her big mouth.(and mine) they were doing a real slow dance and I yelled "go, baby!" and she started laughing like a retarded dolphin. the next week I went to see "bareffoott in the park with Becky, and that was a real good show...not dirty or anything, nooooo, sir!

Shultz, Red, and me have almost all our classes together . Me and shultz(sherri) are substitute teachers for primary,.

I am going to have a birthday party on my birthday and I can hardly wai t!!!! Imagine....15 years this world has beenblessed without even knowing it..15

15 years of cruel labor in the salt mines.. 15 years of mistreatment andhate 15 wonderful years of life and I mean that literally.I love life and each day brings new exitments and new things to discoverlike homework, homework, and homework. Oh well when I'm ri ch and famous I'LL be glad I slaved my life away when I was in the prime of my life .

well, I must be going as I have a DATE with Rock Hudson.

                        SEE YOU, AND MAY YOU FIND TRUE HAPPINESS
                    SUCH AS I IN YOUR JOURNEY THROUGH THIS WONDERFUL L'
        LIFE AND JOY   OF OURS

CHAPTER

8

My dad loved comedy about as much as anyone ever has, and when the comedian would appear on Ed Sullivan, Dad would call for all of us kids: "Comedian, comedian," the siren would blare of the Barr family. Daddy, while we watched, would pass down his Rashi-like commentary on the comedic texts. He would say, "Christ, this guy ain't no comedian, he's a comic, he has absolutely nothing to say, he's an asshole with a couple of jokes."

We would all nod our heads, because we knew that nobody on earth knew more about comedy than our dad, who would play the comedy records to us, and explain all the jokes, half of which I didn't get until I was older.

Every so often, Ed would have on a good comedian, like Jackie Vernon, who me and Daddy really liked. Vernon was, Dad said, a comedic genius, because he had invented a character every man could identify with. He liked all the women comics, too; especially Moms Mabley, and Totie Fields and Phyllis Diller. Comedy, he told me, is funniest when it's about speaking up for the little man or killing sacred cows.

After I had been on the "The Tonight Show" a couple of times, *People* magazine came out to Las Vegas (where I was opening for the Pointer Sisters) and interviewed me. My Mom and Dad were sitting there, and the reporter was listening to me say that my father taught me all about timing, and jokes. Mama said "Why don't you tell Roseanne about what you wrote on your high school graduation thesis?" Daddy said "Why? It's stupid, it's nothing." Now, I really wanted to know, I asked, "What did you put, Dad?" Then Mother answered, because parents, especially Jewish parents, make the other one speak for them. Mother said, "His high school thesis was all about how he wanted to become a stand-up comic after he got out of school."

I looked into my Dad's eyes, and he looked into mine, and it took only one-tenth of a second for us to say, silently, and me first, "You made me a comedian," and his eyes said "Yes, and I made you a good one."

CHAPTER

9

I checked into the Hyatt on Sunset for three days to write in peace. I look out the window and there's The Comedy Store, and I realize with a sinking feeling that it was in this hotel that that comic threw himself to his death on top of (CS owner) Mitzi Shore's car, leaving a note that said he had no future, or something like that. I turn on the TV and there's a John Belushi movie; and I go, sometimes the symbolism just gets to be too much. Then I think of this other comic friend of mine, Don, who called me to say that he was hospitalized last April 'cause he had just gone off the deep end. He had started to think that everything in the world was connected; once he had a dream about arrows and the next day, he was walking down the street and he saw an arrow floating in the gutter. (I paused and said "You mean there's something wrong with that?") He thought that those things signaled the apocalypse, and that he was the only human on earth that could clearly see the signs.

Then I went into a blind panic, because I always feel that way, and I thought I had better talk to someone. I'm really nervous over any sign that I might be going off mentally, that's my number one neurosis. So I did my usual thing, go to libraries and check out books on multiple personality and abnormalities of all kinds. I'm completely panicked now, but then I remember that Don also told me that why my friends love me is because I'm so neurotic, like Woody Allen he says, and then I feel good, because Woody Allen is still alive, crazy as hell and making wonderful movies, fathering babies, walking around New York City, and coping. So I can too, I say, 'cause he's my hero.

God, I love Woody Allen. I hope someday I could meet him. Here's my ultimate Woody Allen and me fantasy . . . different from my Mel Gibson and me fantasy . . . oh, I did get to see Mel Gibson once, in a restaurant here, oh my god, I could hardly tear my eyes away from my Care Figuero salad, with all those delicious artichoke hearts and hearts of palm and my own heart, beating madly as I screamed to my girlfriend Karen between clenched teeth . . . "LOOK LOOK it's Mel Gibson" . . . and he smiled, and walked out while the eyes of every female in that place stuck to his ass until he got into his car. It also had this really great mustard and honey dressing.

Anyway, so I'm in New York, and I'm already a bestselling author, and I'm just walking down the street and standing at a red light (like I really was one time and I turned and noticed that Fran Lebowitz was standing next to me, in her cowboy boots with keys hanging from the belt loop of her jeans . . . I like her too, but I didn't say anything, because I'm too shy, instead, I turned to my husband and between clenched teeth muttered . . . "LOOK, LOOK, it's Fran Lebowitz").

Anyway, there's Woody Allen, and he turns to me says, "You're Roseanne Barr, aren't you?" And I say "Yes, and you're Woody Allen," and he says, "I liked your book" (even in my own fantasies

I wouldn't dare have him say, "I loved your book," though I should have that in there, but I like my fantasies to be more angst-filled and real). "Thank you," I say. Then he says, "Would you like to have coffee?" "I'd love to," I say and so we do and he asks me about my political and spiritual opinions, and I'm so happy, because here's the stuff I really like to talk about since I know everything there is to know in these two areas.

Well, he's blown away of course, and says maybe someday we can work together and I say that I'd love that and then he goes, "I'd like to do a movie about a Jewish female person that I fall in love with instead of all the *non*-Jewish females I always do movies about," and I say, "Maybe we could put a black person in one of your movies too," and he says, "That's a remarkable idea, Roseanne." So just while we're sitting there, we outline this movie and then we have this incredible dinner.

We don't have sex in my own fantasy, because of course I'm on my period like I always am when I travel and anyways, my fantasies are never sexual, unless they're all the way sexual from the beginning, like I meet this rough-looking guy in the dark in the back of a warehouse, well, you know. . . .

Anyhow, so we become friends and everything, and we call each other on the phone all the time, but he calls me more than I call him and talks over his ideas for movies and stuff with me, and I just listen and maybe direct a little by telling him that women don't really think that way at all. So it's my fantasy that I'm sharing great ideas with another brilliant mind and also striking a blow for feminism at the same time. The ultimate. Then, of course, he realizes that I am the most brilliant woman on earth at this time, and that it is me and me alone who can really save the world, and he begins to talk about it all the time, giving me all the credibility I lack and helping to elect me Queen. Then of course I do away with nuclear weapons and war and violence, and everyone lives happily ever after, and everyone loves, adores and worships me.

Then I dump him for Mel Gibson, who I meet after dark behind an old warehouse, and well, you know . . . Mel has very little flesh left on his bones a short while later. I'm picking my teeth a lot.

Not only would I eat Mel Gibson, in the literal and figurative sense, I would consume him, I would inhale him, rolling him around my tongue like a fine Rothschild, swallowing slowly, savoring the essence, gnawing it and slobbering with great masticating noises. Yeah, that's just what I would do.

CHAPTER
10

When I was a little girl I used to have a secret wish and it was that one day I would be a gypsy and be able to take a knapsack and travel all over the world, having incredible adventures, making campfires and cooking beans in cans. My cousin, Sharon, lived out in the country by where the trains ran, and we used to go over there on Sundays, and I loved to sleep over because we could go in her backyard and behind the fence, we could see a big old bull grazing, and behind him, the railroad tracks. We used to try to be toreadors, and wave red shorts or shoes at the Bull so that he would charge at us, we always looked for stuff that would make us scream and run. Occasionally the bull would raise his head, look very bored and swish his tail around to swat flies. He never had steam come out of his nose or had his eyes turn devilish red, like we saw in a cartoon. It was quite disappointing.

We would say "Train's coming!" and look to the right out over towards where the sky and the land were joined, and every time, there it would be, coming faster and faster and getting bigger and bigger. The noise came up with it, first as a hum, and then as a wind. A low, vibrating wind that filled every inch of the space everywhere you looked. At its zenith point, we were transfixed and transported and transcended somewhere beyond the basic three dimensions.

I rode on a train only once in my life—as a four-year-old girl, from Price, Utah, to Salt Lake City, Utah, with my Mom, who was pregnant with Geraldine. I thought about the baby having a ride inside of Mom inside the train, and the metaphysics of that blew my mind. What awe I felt that day! Why *can* you just sit perfectly still and be hurled through space? Don't anyone try to answer that, either, because its boring, and that's one of those questions you need to just *think* about a lot, and make it a point to never understand.

Once, when Sharon and I were gathering sticks and rocks, we saw a man jump off a train with a bedroll. He was not too old a man, but kind of old, I remember thinking he was about thirty. And that thirty was what's just before ninety. "He's a hobo," my cousin Sharon said. She was older than me so she knew about hobos and all. Her daddy was my daddy's brother, and they were both sitting in the house when we came in and I asked my dad what a hobo was. Daddy said a hobo was a bum that jumped on to trains and rode around and got off when it looked like a good place to jump off. A hobo does not have a job, or a family, he just goes from one town to the next, bumming. What an incredible, exciting idea, I thought then (and still do actually).

The only options opened for girls then were of course mother, secretary or teacher. At least that's what we all thought and were preparing ourselves for. Now, I must say how lucky we are, as women, to live in an age where "Dental Hygienist" has been added to the list.

None of these careers seemed interesting

enough to me, so I planned to be a teacher during the school year, and a hobo during the summer. I remember telling this to Daddy and Uncle Larry. Uncle Larry said what he always said to us kids . . . "Don't you dare say Bullshit until I tell you to say Bullshit, got it kid?" Then we would laugh and laugh because Uncle Larry always made it a point to swear around us, and we truly enjoyed it. Sometimes, Uncle Larry would shake up beers and pops and spray them on the walls or the ceilings. Aunt Ruth, his wife, thought he was the most amusing man on earth, and she never yelled at him, or him at her. She was strange, she came from Philadelphia, and when she'd open a can of beer, she'd say, "Tastes just like warm piss." We loved our cousins, Sharon and Joey Barr, because they were the only other poor Jews in town, and we felt normal around them.

One time Aunt Ruth wanted Uncle Larry to paint her bedroom. So, Uncle Larry went and got a spray gun. He closed the doors to the bedroom, and started to paint. First he wrote Fuck and Shit on the ceiling, in black paint, and then he sprayed all the walls black. Then, he sprayed all the windows black, and after that, the bed, the dresser, the chairs, and the rug. When everyone was allowed to see it, they were stunned. He joined the army after that, taking my best friend and cousin, Sharon, over to Okinawa.

After they moved my Bobbe Fanny, Dad's mom, would take me for long walks out to the railroad tracks, and once she told me a story about how her father (who had died just before I was born) had walked at the age of nine from Kiev, Russia, through Europe, fixing people's shoes, which his father had taught him to do before their whole family was slaughtered, except for Grandpa Joe. Bobbe Fanny told me that when Grandpa Joe got to France, he got a job on a boat and went to South Africa where there was a large Jewish community and he fixed shoes there, too. Finally, when he was seventeen, he came to Ellis Island in America, and from New York, walked to Minnesota, where he met Bobbe's mother, got married, and had Bobbe Fanny. I told Bobbe I wanted to walk all over the world too, and she said maybe some of Grandpa Joe got passed to me.

Some of it did, but my sister, Geraldine, is the one who really has Grandpa Joe inside her. She walks ten or twelve hours a day sometimes, just walks and walks. She went to Paris and walked the whole city, accidentally finding Gertrude Stein's house, and then she went to Jerusalem and walked to Bethlehem.

Once after Bobbe Mary died, we were sorting out her drawers and a picture fell out, a picture of her family, mom and dad, and eight children who never made it out of Lithuania alive, and Geraldine and I could not believe it, but there were two girls with faces that looked exactly like her face, like my face, just staring out at us, looking. And some things just get passed down, I guess, like faces, like eyes, the need to walk, and the stories.

My father was a tad bit paranoid. He said I would never be able to have a bicycle. I asked why not and he said never mind. All of the neighbor kids got bikes and I was so upset. Daddy finally explained to me his reasoning. His best friend had been riding alongside him and they were eating peanuts and a car swerved and hit his friend and when Daddy turned to look at his friend, laying in the street, he saw peanuts coming out of his nose and eyes, as his friend lay there smashed and dead. I told all my friends that's why I couldn't have a bike and of course they all understood. I would go walking along with them, while they rode, and then, about two years later, Mom and Dad started going to marital counseling at the Community Mental Health Center, and Daddy brought me home a bike for my eleventh birthday and taught me how to ride it. He made me promise that I would walk across the streets which I agreed to and then never did.

Once I had wheels, I was gone. Having a bike when you are a kid is the most magic experience in the world. That's why I loved that scene in *E.T.* when the bike rises off the ground and Elliott is soaring across the luminous face of the moon. Nothing, not even gravity, can prevent him from saving his friend. That's what having a bike felt like to me, too. I had to make it from my house to the church in less than three minutes, or else the Nazis would win and the world would blow up.

I would escape to NYC; that was the only place on earth where Jews could live, I thought. Also, that's where Ed Sullivan and his show were, which was really where I belonged. Where a Jewish comic shrieked properly for a few moments about living in exile in a cruel, cold world, where the only thing that calmed the terror for a while was the joke, the laugh.

There was a talent contest show in SLC, which was on TV every Sunday afternoon, and you could go on there and if you won, and were good enough, you could eventually go to New York to be on the Ed Sullivan show. The show was hosted by another Jewish person in Utah, Eugene Jelesnic, a fat little man with a bald head and huge nose. Each week, they would showcase four or five people and then the audience would pick the winner. I used to ride my bike downtown, or take a bus, and wait to be discovered by Eugene Jelesnic. I knew that his TV show was broadcast from downtown, and I was sure I would bump into him and that he would discover me.

One day I was riding around with my girlfriend, and who should appear but Mr. TV himself, looking thinner and younger in person I might add. When I saw him I went berserk, screaming, "Mr. Jelesnic, Eugene, my name is Roseanne Barr, and you should discover me, discover me Mr. Jelesnic!" But he just kept walking, like he couldn't hear me. I followed close behind and even beside him for a few blocks, singing and dancing and trying to tell jokes, but alas I was not married yet, and had not hit on the eventual winning combination of myself-and-husband jokes. He continued to stride away from me, and I was shattered; I was too young then to realize that he would merely be the first of many talent-spotting persons to whom I was invisible.

When I met him a few years ago after headlining my own show in SLC, I reminded him of that little girl a long time ago, and he said he couldn't remember anything like that and then he apologized. I forgave him, too, as I always try to do, when someone says they're sorry and were indeed wrong. Never having been wrong myself, it is definitely a trait I admire most in mortals.

Eventually, I did go to NYC, and my first time there I was so high, so in love. My sister and I stayed in the Marriott Marquis, in the Times Square theatre district. I had been flown there to do a private party for a group of accountants and their wives, or what passed as wives. They had seen me on "The Tonight Show," and were going to give me five thousand dollars plus room, board and transportation to come and entertain them. They also sent along a three page letter of their own jokes which were about stock prices and market shares, and accountant type things, which I thought was hysterical, the fact that someone would do that—hire a TV comic and then supply them with jokes.

Oh, NYC—it was bright, beautiful and teeming with the wretched refuse of a million nations, the tired, the poor, the huddled masses yearning to breathe free, and even the homeless and the tempest-tossed were there and it was just so perfect. The first night, Sis and I went to see Lily Tomlin in her show, and we had my manager set it up with her that we could go backstage and meet her. All day long I planned and paced, what would we wear, what would we say. Well, I insisted on dressing up, because I thought that's what you should do when you go to the theatre, so I insisted that sis wear one of my black silk dresses but she instead chose the pink silk dress with hundreds of rhinestones on it. I wore the black, well, we went to the show and everyone else was wearing jeans. I asked Sis, "Why must we always be from Utah?" Doing or dressing or saying the wrong stuff in an effort to rise above our class, we succeed only in making it more *obvious*.

Well, we were too mortified by our clothing to meet Ms. Tomlin, and so we just left. But, I loved your show Lily, and I think that you are a brilliant comic as well as actress.

So, the next night, I went to do the accountant gig. All the accountants looked alike, too, and Sis explained to me that that was because all accountants ever think about is having perfect teeth, getting them capped. So that was why they do things like write comic material and then present you with it, along with a crystal apple engraved with the name of their company on it, like you would keep it, you know, which I did, by the way, because it's so funny.

They hooted and hollered for me as I took the stage, so I felt good, because this is how a comic's mind works . . . this is what is happening behind the jokes you are telling, when you're in that remarkable state of mind that allows you to think six things all at once (it only happens on stage). No, really, it happens when you are in "in character" I guess, because I can do it on interviews too, but anyway. . . .

I'm standing there and I'm thinking, "They know who I am, good, I won't have to work hard to win them over." I tell a few jokes. The laughs keep decreasing, rather than building. Something's wrong. Usually, it's my timing's off, my attitude's off or I'm bored and not focused into the act enough. I make the necessary adjustments. Still nothing. After twenty minutes of it, I get that mixture of terror/relief that comics get sometimes, when they realize that this one is all the audience's fault (which happens very very rarely) and no comic even likes to admit that the crowd would ever be beyond their control. Even the wives didn't laugh, and Jesus, you'd think that if you had to be married to one of these joes, what with the numbers and anal retention and dazzling smiles you'd be busting a goddam gut, but no, these were the good wives, the Stepford types you know—wives on drugs and psychotherapy. A room full of hey guys! and honeys! Whew.

So, I'm thinking, what the hell do I do? So then I pull out the papers, the ones they gave me with the jokes about the stocks and the shares and shit, and I start reading it off. The room comes alive, no, it explodes; it roars, it throws back its collective head and howls. I continue reading the jokes. Finally I say, to myself, I've got them, and now I move in for the kill. I'm two minutes away from the closer, my run of four jokes that are so funny they always work anywhere. I figured I'll end big. But no; the minute I go into my stuff, the room is silent and the roar dies down and that's it. Polite applause, man.

The next day they cancelled my suite, left me and Sis in one room together and avoided looking at me in the elevators. I asked them to pay me in cash.

I got to ride the ferry into the harbor and see the Statue of Liberty which really blew my mind, and Ellis Island, because here were the things that almost all of my relatives had seen in their first glimpse of the new land, and it had the effect on me where I could not stop the redness around my nose and eyes and the tears running down my face. I looked at Sis, she was the same, as was my husband later, thinking about Scotsmen and Irishmen and home. Everyone cries when they see the Statue of Liberty, because she is so beautiful and powerful and means so many wonderful things to so many people. To all who came from Europe, she is the symbol of the womb, of motherhood, protection, justice and peace. To accountants, though, I think they just admire her teeth, and their wives just think she's a Dear!

New York City is a place to which I return over and over and over again because it is a place that makes me tell stories. I found it in a great state of disrepair, very old and crumbly where you couldn't tell the difference between the smell of old wine and new piss. I felt like a new immigrant there, like I had just arrived in a foreign city and didn't know its language or customs yet. I had heard via TV and such about the staggering indifference of the residents there and their very carnal and crass way of dealing with others—particularly strangers. I guess I had the picture of opium dens and heroin addicts with punk hairdos crawling around.

Actually I was very surprised by the fact that although there is very little civility there (which I loathe anyway as a false class-issue), these are the friendliest folk on earth. If they don't want to talk to you, they don't, unlike other places where they don't want to talk to you and *do,* in a manner that makes you hate them. How very much more kind to instead, without pretense, just walk away.

The people who choose to talk to you there always have the greatest and highest senses of humor, and seem so empathetic to your condition of being lost in New York and eager to help initiate you into its culture. The only really rude people were the ones at restaurants and in service positions who all came from Iowa (and other places like that) and thought, by being rude, they were assimilating—but what they were attempting to assimilate into is a person from Iowa's impression of New York, kind of once removed—like the way men talk about childbirth. Try to avoid people from Iowa in NYC. You can easily recognize them as they are not ETHNIC.

Other people are so vibrant and alive and short there . . . they all hang around delis and drive cabs and smoke a lot. These are the interesting people. The great ethnic folk of NYC are the ones I like to watch, follow, talk to and eat with. They do everything in a noisy fashion, which those obsessed with civility I'm sure regard as rude. I imagine that everyone in NYC loves to fuck, and they don't consider it a chore, either—but another wonderful excuse to make loud noises.

I of course rode the subways at night, sat next to mean-looking black youths in my fur coat and my diamond ring, and told them that I was a tourist here and just out wandering aimlessly. They would counter with wonderful suggestions about where to eat and what to go see, and I would disembark and wander Times Square with 3,000 dollars tucked into my brassiere feeling rich and very very safe. Even my husband, who is Protestant and therefore paranoid, said he never in his life felt safer anywhere else. When we once went to NYC together, we walked around at night all dressed for the occasion, Bill in a trench coat, scarf and hat and me in a fur coat—we looked like a reporter with a rich Jewish refugee. I liked going there with Bill and I liked going there with my sister and I liked going there alone, which made for three different New York Cities. I know others have said they did not fare as well as I there, but they must have been putting out those fear vibes, which can be deadly. You must never be afraid in New York City, because then you will call bad stuff to you and you will not like it there.

It is, above all else, a lovely and wonderful place to be fat . . . which I of course loved. Even thin people look fat there, and fat women are always out with handsome men (not like in California, where everyone thinks fat is something you can catch, and therefore is to be avoided). New York has wonderfully beautiful fat people, just the way fat people should be, happy and healthy and sexy looking.

The men there look just the way you have always imagined that men should look . . . like they do an honest and hard-working day's work, then come home, remove their leather jackets, stroke and listen to children, fix a sandwich and go to sleep with you and snore, and if there is any noise at all during the night, could get up and take care of it, like a man, like what men are for, loud and lusty and constantly on guard, sweet and dumb and playful. Real Men. Why, it was enough to remember why you like them in the first place. Not the kind of men you see in the Pentagon, or in politics or on TV evangelist shows, or the kind of men that you see in the movies or on TV either, but real men who smell not too clean and never wonder more than they should if their penis is too short—and I just know it never is. Really wonderful men who always talk about their mothers and grandmothers with respect and love, rather than patronizingly about their mother's and grandmother's love for them.

It's just a damn shame sometimes that I'm married and that there's AIDS, 'cause if there wasn't I would rip through that town like a she-devil hurricane until I got tired, which would be a long, long time. Oh well.

But even more sensual and exuberant than that, New York is a place where it is lovely and correct to use the word "Fuck."

They pronounce it different, there, they say "FOCK," with an "o." And the word has various meanings—it can mean

1. Hello, how are you?
2. Move over
3. That's funny
4. How sweet of you
5. I'm busy
6. What are you? An idiot?

And many more things.

I love it when men say "fock" in New York, and I love it when they say it to me in NY.

The nicest thing in the world happened to me in New York City. I was trying to escape from the tabloid assholes, feeling very unsafe and invaded on the streets. A man drove up and rolled down his window and said to me: "Roseanne, we are all so proud of you, honey! Hang in there!" He made me feel so happy, so I wanted to say thanks. People in New York treat me like I'm a human being first and a celebrity second—and I like that so much more.

CHAPTER
11

I was on my way to school walking up this huge hill. The hill was so steep that sometimes when you would walk home in the winter, if you lost your footing even for A SECOND, you would ski down and crash in a heap at the bottom. It was dangerous coming down it in winter, and treacherous going up it in any weather. It was the longest most ominous hill there ever was, and it made your calves burn and the balls of your feet ache when you zenithed.

I was up there, this one day, that day, the big day, with my girlfriend Sherri Ann Smith, and we were wearing our twin outfits that we had sewed in Home Ec. Being twins or looking like them, or dressing like twins, is and was a big thing in Utah. I don't know why, and don't care to think about why, either, because anytime I start to try to think about ANYTHING in Utah, I always figure it out, and then I am terrifically bored out of my skull, that things mysterious are all stupid childish and so predictable in that state of mind, the state of Utah.

So, we are crossing the street, dressed like twins, at about 8:40 A.M. and I remember standing on the corner and looking down the hill and up the street, looking for cars, and then we stepped off the curb and kind of jaywalked a little bit, not too much out of the walk way (which I have to say now, because our Utah lawyer settled my case out of court when the opposition said, two years later, that I had been walking down the middle of the street, begging cars to hit me. The truth is, that I did not do that until a year after the car hit me, when I went nuts).

After I went nuts, I went to the Utah state hospital for almost a year. The lady who hit me's lawyers used my subsequent going nuts against me and were able to only have to shell out twelve hundred bucks in settlement court, or whatever the fuck you call it. But anyways, I wasn't ever nuts until after I got hit by the car. I hate all lawyers (as well as doctors, headshrinkers, social workers, and all other assholes whose job it is to fuck with people's will, minds, and sense of truth). I didn't feel this way until I went nuts, either. I didn't go nuts until I got hit by that car, Mom. OK.

I was fine till then, Mom says all the time. I was just fine until I got hit by that car and went nuts. Just fine. That cracks me up, man. When I was just fine, I was really out there, you know, I was so far out there that I really believed that God was on our side, or that I was on the same side as God. That world, let me assure you, is, I feel the really schizonutso dead not right in the head place.

I was out of that world called Normal for a very long time, and occasionally I slip back even now.

I do not choose to live there, however, because it is just too damn boring and since I subsequently and clear-headedly have chosen to attempt to think freely, I choose to remain nuts, on the other side of the mirror. I can see my reflection more clearly and my scars are not ugly after all, but, rather badges of courage, gleaned from a frightening journey out of and away from a foreign country/soul where I never really belonged.

I can go back to Normalsville and am often dragged back there for people who require constant clarification. This is apparently what they want to know:

1. How nuts is nuts?
2. Whats the difference between nuts and neurotic?
3. Are you dangerous?
4. Do you ever feel frightened, at the way you think?

If you are Normal, the answers are all No.
If you are Nuts, the answers are all Yes.
I try not to lose too much in the translation.
I try not to be drained too much at having to explain.
I try not to scream, weep, moan, and howl at how far away everything and everybody is.
I try not to laugh too much knowing that I am your audience, you are not mine.
How deeply I see you see me.
How clearly I hear you listen.
How entertaining I find your entertainment.
How transfixed I am at the sight of you watching ME bite the various heads off assorted chickens.
I am this year's Geek, and might I say I am humbled and grateful for the honor.

I have been paid well.

As if money would make everything right. As if money could compensate for all that pain, but people think it does. That's why they don't have any money, too. That really is the biggest joke of all to me now, the scariest shit of all, and I really do think about it all the time. The way people with money think about money as opposed to people who don't have any money, and the way they think about money. I've been both. When you don't have any money, you try to be OK without it. When you do have money, you try to be OK having it, and all the time you try to tell yourself you'd be OK again if you lost it.

If you don't have a lot of money, you think that people who do are luckier and happier than you are. When you do have money, you think that something's wrong with you because you're not happier or luckier than you were before you had it. It's really two sides of the same coin for me. No, money don't make ya happy, it's really true, you regular folk out there. I'm tellin ya. It don't make ya happy, but then being poor or broke don't make you happy either.

I think you get money to come to you when you realize that either way, it doesn't matter. I believe that the Universe rewards you when you leave the sane world and jump out into pure nonsensical creativity. But, then, I'm nuts, remember.

Being nuts is its own reward. You get to jet right off of planet earth and see colors, things, people, time, space, energy fields, life itself in a much more positive way. In the nuts world, you know exactly what it would take to fix, save, conquer, rule, or lead the world. All nuts people know how to do this. The problem is, as soon as they say they do, the mindwashers and head doctors come and get them and they put them away, drug them, tie them up, try to cut out parts of their brains, hook them up to "heart attack machines," etc., until they come back to their "senses." That's just what they do now, to the nuts. They used to do worse; bleed them, imprison them, burn them at the stake (they estimate nine million of them were burned at the stake over a couple hundred years). They try to kill, or silence everyone who says they know how to save the world. You might be one who does know, but you're not really in any danger, unless you *tell* them that you know. That's how they figure that you're nuts, you tell them that you know how to save the world. Then they'll get you, unless you're particularly clever about it, and say that you're a poet, songwriter, writer, comedian, storyteller, artist, or whatever. Then they will tolerate you, because they'll just think you're controllable, because you obviously still care about money. And when you still care about money, you're part of the world. You don't really want to save it—you're OK.

Because these other type of "sane" folk, don't want the world saved, they want it good and dead, all of it, and everything in it. They want it tidy, too. All catalogued and tidy and dead, like museums. Like when you go into the museums and they have pictures of Indians in there, and wall mountings and stories that say how the Indians lived before they became extinct. Their pottery is there, their ceremonial costumes, their pipes, shoes, totem gods, but if you are appalled and scared, because you want the Indians back, the living Indians back, well, you just ain't right in the head.

You can tell that people in the sane world want everything dead: They support war over peace every time. They support force over compromise every time. They go to their churches and synagogues and mosques and pray to their dead, totemic gods to help them make it through the night a few more years, till they can rest, at last, when they're at peace, when they are in the good place, heaven, and finally, good and dead. Necropolis.

I want to live. I choose Life. I don't wanna hate nobody. I wanna be nuts.

When I was sixteen, I was walking to school, I had knowledge stored in my head. I knew that America was the greatest country on earth, I feared the way communists think, and that they might be out to get me. I also feared people who were not mormon, because, well, they couldn't be saved, and probably were all child molesters, murderers, etc. I wanted to be a hairdresser/teacher/housewife, I wanted to be a mother. I thought being a mother meant taking care of children. I thought I would never find the right guy who really loved me, 'cause I was fat. I believed that when I died I would go to heaven and see God, and I believed that black men had bigger weenies. I was normal, not nuts at all, not paranoid, just naive, not delusional, just young. That's what they would say, you know.

This car hit me. I didn't even see it coming. I was thrown up into the air, and came down on the hood, where the ornament went into my head.

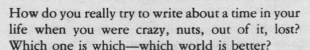

How do you really try to write about a time in your life when you were crazy, nuts, out of it, lost? Which one is which—which world is better?

I think the best way is to think about it as being another, a kind of a distant and misty place, surrounded by fog that rolls in and rolls out of your memory every now and then. Especially when you are all alone, and it's night time, and you're in some hotel room, in a strange city, opening for Julio Iglesias. Being "sane" is like being off balance a little; it's just like one part of your brain takes over and gets a little bit bigger than the other parts. You can really feel the parts of your brain when you're nuts, too. You know that you can really function the way that people in the regular world do, but it really bores you to think that you might have to. I wasn't the chemical kind of nuts, or the mentally ill kind of nuts, or the dangerous kind of nuts, not schizo, or nothin' like that, Jack. I was part of the normal world where everything bad that has ever happened to you is blamed on you. When you are told over and over again, sometimes by people who are paid to help you that maybe it happened to you, well, because you wanted it to, somehow. Because you asked for it, or that's what you get when you . . . rock the boat, go out looking for some trouble, mouth off, think you know everything, disrespect the law, your elders, the rules. The kind of world where you're always told that you might actually desire being hurt, humiliated, beaten, raped, left. Because, you don't think you're good enough, or that you think you don't deserve better, the kind of world where you are told all your life not to be independent, but to belong, not to fight, but conform. The kind of world where you actually believe that what happens to you happens in a chaotic nonsensical fashion, out of the son of a bitch bad luck, instead of the truth which is that all that happens to you happens to you because it is systematically, politically, religiously planned like that, to be that way. When everything starts to appear to you as if it has been planned that way, that you don't deserve it, that you don't want it, that it has been forced on you, you go nuts. Nuts is a disease of women. Nuts is the truth. Nuts is a Revolution. Quoting now from the Book of Revolutions I by R. Barr: Know ye the truth and the truth shall make you nuts.

That it would ever make you free is the biggest hunk of slanderous shit that ever came down the pike. I went nuts, and sometimes I can pretend like I came back. I probably would have remained "sane" (I like what comic Robin Tyler calls it, "insane and outsane") and never gone off the deep end, off the edge, into the abyss, off my rocker, out of my tree, off my nut, if I would never have been hit by the car. So, I guess that's how I start to tell this story, that when I was sixteen, I got run over by a car. There.

After the accident, I had a lot of trouble focusing and remembering things. I had always been an "A" student, and now suddenly, the concept of math began to fade and I couldn't understand it anymore.

But I began to write poetry then. Weird poetry that I really couldn't understand. It would all just come pouring out, as if I were in a trance, and not until I re-read it did I know what it was about.

Sometimes it would scare me to read it, because it seemed to belong to another place and time and, I would wonder "where did I get this?"

> *guilt blame*
> *arms legs*
> > *bones*
>
> *birth murder*
> *sunlight in graveyards*
> > *Look!*
>
> *Walk stumble*
> *pathway on fire*
> > *movement*
>
> *Vows of deception*
> > *blood*
> > *ashes*
> > *a dome of ashes*
>
> *Falling off*
> > *falling away*
> > *tongues in the dirt*
>
> *Go to the Light!*
> > *children first*
> > *helpless*
> > *Big yellow moon*
> > *We fly away . . .*

Almost every night after the accident, I would

dream that I could not wake up. I was in bed trying to move even an eyelid, screaming at my paralyzed body to open its eyes. I was horrified that people would think I was dead and bury me alive. I tried, within the dream to telepathically call for someone to come and wake me. But they would never hear me screaming.

I was afraid to sleep, and sometimes I would make it for days without it. Once, I hadn't slept for several days, and was sitting in my mother's living room where my eyes rolled back and I went into convulsions. I think this is when Mama started to think about having me hospitalized.

Hospitalizing me helped me, unwittingly, because of the drugs I was given. I was able to sleep very well there at night. As soon as I came out of the hospital, and went off the Melaril, the dream came back.

One night, while in the dream, I started to talk to myself. I said, "This is only a dream, you will wake up, because you always have. This is your brain trying to heal itself from the injury. You're remembering being unconscious, and not being able to wake up." Then I was able to start moving parts of the dream around. I found that if I counted to five, I could wake up, partly. As the fog cleared, and I counted to five again, I could awaken all the way. Soon, I was able to go inside of all my dreams, change or understand them, and then I could sleep. Sometimes I have tried to bring things from the sleep world back with me, for instance, in my dream red dress means money.

Anyway, at this time I started my obsession with fives. Everything had to count out to five or something terrible would happen. At times, people, engaging me in conversation, would stop talking, and ask why my fingers, lips, and eyes were moving spasmodically. I could not explain that I was metering their words and adding or subtracting syllables to make my rule of fives.

One time I was with a friend of mine, Pam Matteson, a comedian, when she started to tell how she had to make everything come out nine times.

She was opening for Rodney Dangerfield and he told us that a lot, most, performers, creative types have number obsessions, so I've felt less crazy since then.

Sometimes, when I see him, Rodney asks if I've been busy, what with all my career shit, and trying to fit twelve words on each finger. I laugh and laugh

Show biz is a great haven for weirdos like me.

Later in my life, at about twenty-eight, I experienced the whole dream again and parts of it afterward.

I believe my brain was healing itself from the concussion of the accident.

Now, I also believe that I had gone somewhere else, somewhere so far inside of myself, almost back to Mammalian Memory. I hear other people talk about experiencing like things, but they usually say they think they saw God in Heaven. I didn't see God, but I do believe I figured out for myself what God is, and what death is.

I believe, for myself, that all the myths and stories about death are really the unconscious reliving of birth.

I believe that our births are the most traumatic experiences of life.

For, when we began to be expelled from our mothers wombs, we feel that we are dying and leaving "Heaven," "Paradise."

The tunnel we hear people tell about is our memory of the vagina, and the light we go towards is the light of the world.

You are born, and you are separated from The Garden of Eden, and you will ache from that separation all of your life.

The first time you are put to your mother's breasts, you are healed with Mannah from Heaven, the perfect food. The first time you are held in your mother's arms, you unconsciously perceive the arms and the face of God. All myth speaks only of the "Arms and Face of God." These politics of separation are where, I believe, we get all our myths, and all of our ethics.

The world's first religion celebrated the fact that things died and are reborn. We didn't believe that we had "dominion over" the beasts and the earth, we believed we were part of them, we *were* part of them.

It was a religion that believed in cycles, in nature, in birth. By woman you were born onto this earth, the Great Mother, and when you die you will become part of her again.

We had this big TV room where all the nuts used to sit to watch TV and right next to them was a room with all the Mormon lady attendants quilting. I lived on a floor with three other girls, one was twelve, one was fourteen and one was like fifteen, and the rest were all crazy asshole adults. One time Suggy said "Can you cut my hair, man, cut my bangs for me?" Sure I'll cut your bangs. So I go in this room and I trim her bangs up real pretty for her and she grabs the scissors out of my hand. "I'll kill you—look what you've done to my hair!" and she came at me with the scissors.

Once in a while we would be let out. On Thursdays, we'd always go see "The Computer Wore Tennis Shoes." We went to see that movie every week 'cause that was the only one they'd take us to, the rest weren't socially acceptable. They had a nasty word or something. So I saw "The Computer Wore Tennis Shoes" about nine times.

One time I was eating my lunch at the commissary; macaroni and cheese, white bread, mashed potatoes, corn, and a glass of milk. I dropped my fork, so I bent down to pick it up and I look across and Clare was sitting there with no crotch in his pants, it was all cut out and his balls were hanging out. I find a huge caterpillar worm in my food so I go change it, 'cause that was no big deal, then I go, "Clare, man, you gotta have somebody sew up your pants, and you gotta wear underwear cause you know, all your shit is hangin out," and he's sitting next to this other guy who's like younger— they always sit together, and this younger guy looks like someone put his head in a vise and squeezed it about four inches too short, so that his nose and face were way out in front plus his head was very little, and Clare goes, "Go ahead and tell her." He says "Are you sure you want me to tell her?" Clare goes, "Yeah, go ahead and tell her" and he goes,

"Well Clare cuts his pants out on purpose." I go, how come? He looks to Clare and Clare goes "Yeah, go ahead, she can deal, you can tell her." "Because he is a woman trapped in a man's body."

Debbie would walk in very slow motion. It would take her eight hours to go from one end of the room to the other. First she'd tilt her head this way then she'd tilt her head that way to look both ways, then her arms would go up then her leg would go out then it would go down then the weight under her hips would shift from back to forward, and that was like one step, then she'd look both ways and repeat it, and no one paid attention to her. Then one day she just walked—you know, like a person, and everyone stood up and clapped *"Yeah* Debbie," and then she never slowed down, she just kept getting faster, until she was walking back and forth, wall to wall eight hundred times a day. And then her speech came up like that too; when she started walking the speech came slowly, and then it was normal, "Hi, how are you," then it went faster and faster and faster, then it went to "I hate you," and then they came and took her away for a few weeks, then she came back and was doing that very slow number again. She was like a doll, malfunctioning, and then taken to the doll factory and fixed.

We used to go on panels to all the schools with social workers around every college in Utah and we'd talk to them. The doctor would come with us, and he'd go "Well, we're here to talk about mental illness in youth, and these are our four panel members." First it would be David, or whatever his name was (who'd killed his parents because they didn't like his girlfriend). He'd go, "My name is David, and I'm in here for family problems." I thought this was just great and then Lynn would go, "My name is Lynn and I'm sixteen but something happened when I was a baby, so I'm really only twelve." And then I'd go, "My name is Roseanne and I'm in here for heroin addiction." They'd ask me drug questions but luckily there were other kids in there for drugs so I just used all their language—"yeah, I was shooting crystal and meth"—they had no idea why I was in there. We went to a town one time and I go "I'm in here cause I'm psychotic," and the doctor goes, "No one on our panel is psychotic Roseanne." I go, *"Then why am I in here?"* And the other panel members roared laughing. This was my first stand-up routine.

I never did do drugs. I was too afraid. I knew I was already so far out and away from "reality" that I didn't want to push it even farther.

The problem with drugs, as I have always believed, is that if you take them, you will believe that you are on them, and that is a great excuse to erase your own responsibility
culpability
ability
and
life.

One time I was at home—a Utah nut on a weekend visit home from the nuthouse—and this guy in the neighborhood, Sandy, kept trying to have sex with me. He said, "Let's smoke some pot and do what comes naturally." So I'm just being a hippie all the way, a cook chick, the whole sixties thing; and since it was Utah it was shocking—and that made it fun. I had smoked maybe two times in high school and nothing happened, so I thought I was highly evolved and wouldn't feel anything this time either. So I'm sitting in Sandy's apartment, smoking pot, looking around—and everything suddenly looks interesting. The ceiling is intensely interesting. The cracks in the ceiling are incredible.

My eyes are whirling around and my mouth is gaping open, and he says, "What's the matter with you?," "Nothing, nothing, why, does it seem like anything's the matter?" He goes, "Have you ever been high before?," and I go, "Of course!" Then we start having sex on the couch, just foreplay, and I was really getting into it too, which was amazing for me. We went to the bedroom and fucked then; I still didn't know what you were supposed to do. I thought of something like an article from *Seventeen*. "Why, what you do Roseanne is you lay there poised, and smile." So I'm with this guy and I'm smiling at him like this: I tilt my head to one side, then to the other, as if I'm saying: "My, aren't you doing a very good job. You're so intelligent to have figured that out." Immediately afterward, I pulled my dress down from over my head, and a wave of paranoia hit that almost knocked me through the wall. I said, "You know, I've just remembered something," and he says "What?" I said, "I've just got to get to my room." He goes "Is anything the matter?" "No." I say "But it is very important that I go into my room now." He says, "Okay. See Yah." The sensitive guy that he was. So I'm going and thinking, Mom and Dad are going to see that you're stoned, and your ass is going to be a piece of shit.

You had better get up in that room and go to sleep or something so that they don't find out because you'll lose everything—you'll lose your whole weekend. And losing your weekends was so bad. That's how we talked then. Every place has its own language, and so *weekends* were very important.

I've got to get up to that room, and I don't want Mom and Dad to see me. I take three steps into the house, and the familiar oppression of my family started to close in on me, thick, rusty, and smelling like ketchup.

I'm in the kitchen, and I hear Mom and Daddy come in from outside and I think, They are going to see you, and they're going to know. They will then send you back to the nuthouse and take away your weekends. Here's what you do: Daddy will go over and he'll turn on the TV and then he'll go take a shit, like he always does, and Mom will go into the bathroom near her bedroom, so you just stand here and be very quiet and they won't see you. I'm counting out the steps, one, two, three, now he's at the TV, step, step, step, now he's in the bathroom; Mom's in her bath, and I fuckin' dash up them steps, and I hit the door with the glass window in it and I slam it so hard that the glass shatters all over the floor.

Imagine Mom's head coming in the window and craning all the way around the corner looking at me, finding me masturbating. Oh no, she's going to come with her long neck and stretch it to find me in here, and then she'll say, "Hi Honey," and then she'll come in and then she'll smell the smoke on my breath and she'll know that I'm stoned. So I look over and I have this bottle of Prince Houbigant perfume on the dresser that the lady who ran over me in the car gave me. I knew it was real expensive stuff, about seven bucks. I go over there and take a *huge* swig of it and then I get sick. I get so sick I run into the bathroom, throw water in my mouth, spitting, and then run back into the room and close the door and go to sleep. Just go in here and go to sleep and you'll wake up and everything will be fine. But I'm freaking out: Daddy's at the bottom of the stairs, "Are you laying up there on your ass? Roseanne, are you laying on your ass?" I go, "Yes," "Well goddammit, blah, blah, blah." He's gonna turn on the TV, and he's gonna lay down on the floor, he won't hear nothing. Get out of this house, Get out of this house, run for your life! Already being extremely paranoid, and compounding it with a pot high, was probably not the best thing for a girl home from the nuthouse on a weekend furlough. I was living half in and half out of the mirror world, anyway, normally, and the drug made everything so much more frightening and unreal.

I ran out into the park and started thinking: I am not in the park, I'm still at home in my bed, no you're not, you're in the park, no you're home in bed thinking you're in the park and I just didn't know what was true so I went over to this tree and I go, now run your hand along the bark. So I take my hands and I just *gouge* them down the tree and my palms are bleeding. I go, good, blood, that means I'm in the park. I see these Mormon Girls and they are playing volleyball or some other Mormon Girl kind of thing, and I go, They will see you standing here and they will know you are stoned and they will take away your weekends. And then I think those girls will help me, and I went up to them, and I go "Excuse me," and they go, "Yes," and I go "Are you LDS?" and they say "Uh Huh," and I go "Well I'm LDS too, do you live around here?" They said they lived across the street and I go, "Could we please go over to your house? I have taken a lot of drugs. I'm never taking drugs again as long as I live. I have already asked God to forgive me, and he has spoken to me saying, Asketh ye, these girls playing volleyball and therein ye shall find comfort!" That's how folks talk in Utah and they are not on drugs. "I just need to get OK from this drug and I swear, I'm never going to do it again, but I can't think right, I need to go and sit somewhere, please help me," and they go, "OK."

So we go over there and they start talking to me like Mormons would. Why did you take these drugs? I go "Please, Please don't say anything to me, I really can't talk right now. Please don't say anything to me. I swear, I'll call you guys when I'm better, and I'll talk about the whole thing with you, but please don't talk to me now." And they go, "OK." Then I'm sitting there thinking, extremely paranoid, my hands bloody, "They have guns, like all Mormons have guns. You are so out of control that you are going to say something to make them go and get their gun and kill you, because I know you, you always do that, you are out of control and you won't be able to stop yourself." I am imagining the things that I could say to get myself killed, like "I am a *Communist* you know!" or "I'm really a *Satan* worshipper and I just wanted to come into your house so I could destroy you!!" The third one: "I want you all to initiate me into the world of Lesbianism, I want to Fuck *all* of you!" So I think: Oh God, I'm gonna get killed here. I say, "I feel better now, can I use your phone?" I call up Daddy and say: "Could you please come and get me? I'm really really messed up and I've lost my way home." Daddy goes, "Where are you?" "I'm at Liberty Park" (three blocks from our house where I have lived for eighteen years). Daddy goes, "You stay there, we'll be right there." I'm standing in the park and up drives Mother and Father in their station wagon, and they go, "Get in the car, Get in here." They had that look, that panicked look that parents get when their crazy daughter is out loose. I felt myself come down just then. I get into the car and say "I was just joking, I just didn't want to walk home." Daddy goes "Well good."

I went to my room and noticed that my mother had already cleaned up all of the broken glass and I just laid down and went to sleep.

I wake up after my nap and it is five in the morning, the morning was beautiful and I was so thankful that I made it through without getting busted. I wanted to go out for a walk and greet the sunrise in my maxicoat. I walked back down to the park and I'm telling myself, "You're going to be OK, nobody found out you'd gotten high . . ." I'm calming myself down. Up pulls this car and a woman gets out, "What are you doing?" "Would'st thou helpeth me?" She goes, "Would

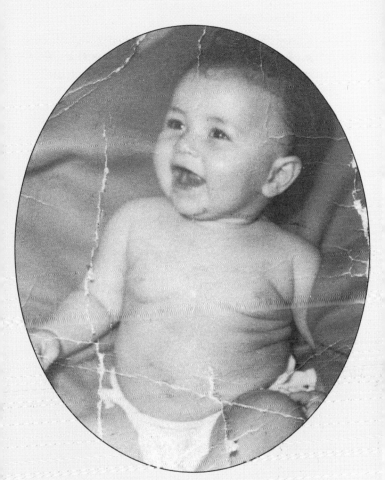

Roseanne at ten months old.

Roseanne. The early philosopher.

Mrs. Jones said that Roseanne's three-month-old cousin was "such a smart baby." Roseanne asked, "What did he ever say to make you think he was so smart?" Mrs. Jones called it in to the Salt Lake Tribune. This was Roseanne's first published joke.

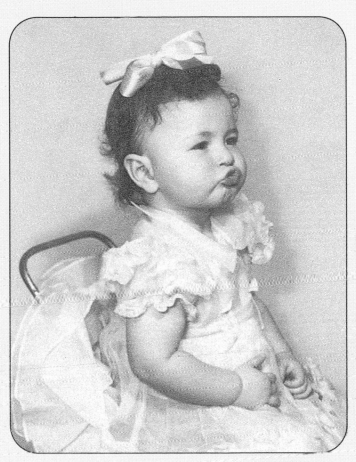

Honing the skills I would need to make it in Hollywood.

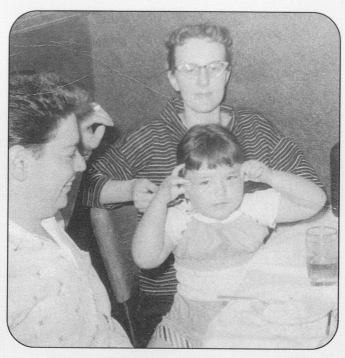

*Roseanne as a "Chinaman," age eighteen months
(Aunt Virginia was thrilled.)*

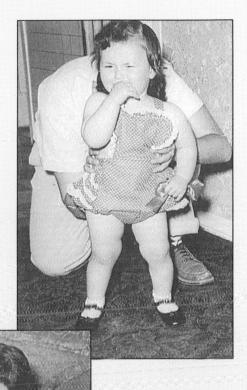

Daddy hiding from photographers.

Roseanne contemplating, "How do I get out of this town and live well?"

Roseanne with her favorite doll, "Judy the walking doll," whose head she later drilled holes into with Dad's power tool.

Roseanne napping with her Uncle Perry.

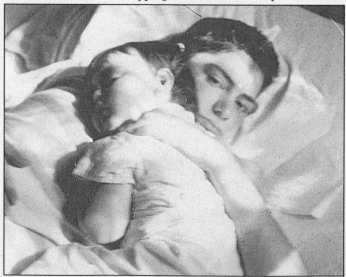

Roseanne with Joanne and Binky, who called her babysitter Robbie a BITCH.

"*I*'ll be leaving Utah soon."

Roseanne and Geraldine, hairdos by Helen.

The great and terrible Oz. Bobbe Mary!

My parents, before Roseanne (above).

After Roseanne (right).

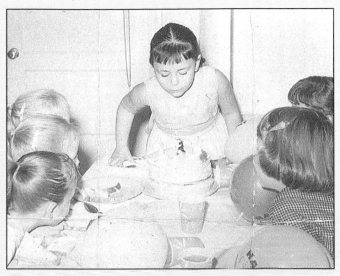

Roseanne's fifth birthday party. Mom says she doesn't really know why we put a witch on the cake.

Roseanne with her Daddy.

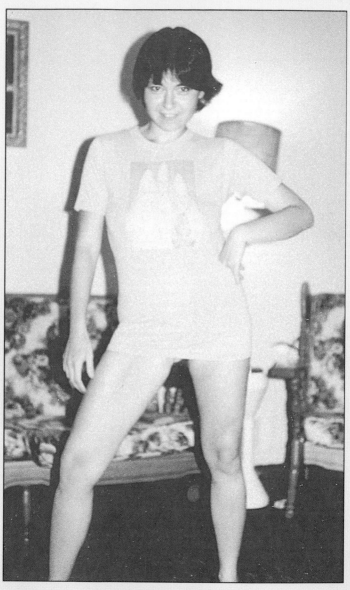

Look what I've done to myself.

The happy couple —"American Gothic."

Halloween in a 600-square-foot house. Denver, Colorado, 1982.

Roseanne and Geraldine, 1987.

Roseanne's children: Jake, Jennifer, Jessica cleaning up their room.

*Roseanne and Dan Conner (John Goodman)
from the TV series "Roseanne." (Copyright © 1989
Capitol Cities/ABC, Inc.; Timothy White)*

you please come in the house and I'm gonna tell my old man that I was out with you all night and that you are just bringing me home. Please, you are saving my life." So I go, "Well, OK." I figure I had gotten lucky, no one had found out about my drug escapade, and now perhaps, I could help someone else to level the Karma, to repay the good with good.

So we walk into her house and there is her house and there is her husband, or her Old Man or whatever he was, with two or three Mexican kids in little T-Shirts and underwear. He is packing a bag, throwing his shit, and she goes, "Hi, I was drinking with Suzy last night and I passed out at her house, so she brought me home." I saw her get out of the car with a man and he goes, "You think I fucking fall for shit, you think I'm going to believe that kind of fucking shit from you, you fucking whore, you're fucking everybody all the Goddamn time, I'm fucking through with you." I don't know what to do, so I sat on the couch. (This story proves that at the time I wasn't mentally OK, I had a reason to be in the nuthouse.)

I hear them in the bedroom arguing more, and I have a vision from the Lord right there, "You can heal these people, Roseanne." So I walk in the bedroom, all ablaze and I go, "Excuse Me." They stop and turn and look at me, and I go "We gotta love each other, man, 'Make Love, Not War, Man' " (said like Dennis Hopper in a maxicoat). But I don't know what to do next, so I just go and sit back on the couch. Then it comes into my head and I return to the bedroom, "If you love a thing, you must let it go," or some other Kahlil Gibran bullshit. The man says, "This is all very nice of you, but, I want you to leave now!!! Get the Fuck out of here, Leave us *alone*." The woman starts screaming that maybe I slipped something into her drink last night. She tells me to Get the Fuck Out. Then she starts crying to the man that she thinks she got drugged at my house and he puts his arms around her. I still applaud that woman's intelligence. Another happy Utah couple! Saved by yours truly.

So I come home singing "Let the Sunshine In." The sun is coming up and there is the police and Mother and Father are going, "We heard you walk out of this house at 5:00, where the hell were you?" I go, "I was just taking a walk." Then they all assured me that everything was going to be just fine, and then Daddy took me back to the nuthouse that night, cause it was Sunday. We had a great talk. But about two days later, they came in and said, "You have lost your weekends. You will not be able to go home for two consecutive weekends." So that's a month, cause you went home every other week. "You will have to stay here, because you were out of control."

I was glad I was not busted for the pot, or I would have lost two months of weekends. It was truly my luck to be busted for helping others.

PART

2

CHAPTER

12

Georgetown, Colorado, was a beautiful little town, nestled high up in the Rocky Mountains, sixty miles west of Denver. You could not go there now and find Georgetown, Colorado, because the place that I'm telling you about doesn't exist anymore, although everyone who lived there could maybe reinvent it, if we were all together, but then perhaps not, because the Time itself could never be again. This is another story about the sixties, which did not begin for me until 1971. I was nineteen years old, had told my parents that I was going to go to Colorado to visit an old girlfriend, Linda Rizzardi, and had saved four hundred dollars from my job as a salad lady at Chuckarama in Salt Lake City to buy a car.

I got fired from my job there because I missed two days due to having a root canal, and since my tooth nerve was exposed, it was rather uncomfortable, to say the least, to work in a walk-in freezer. My Utah dentist removed the nerve over a two-day period, which is probably unheard of, but upon seeing the *Marathon Man* movie, I did not hesitate to make the connection between Nazi torture and Utah medicine. He gave me a prescription for codeine, and because I was just out of the nuthouse and a teenager, my father and mother and he were convinced they must regulate every pill, as perhaps I could become a codeine addict over a two-day period. Screaming in agony for forty-eight hours, my father would not allow me a pain killer. He would say, "You can have another pill in three more hours." I would get down on my knees and pray to my father to either give me a pill now, or let me throw myself in front of a truck, but he would not, because like all people from Utah, he was convinced that doctors and dentists knew best.

Suffice it to say that I was a tad bit depressed because, having just been fired, then the end came with my headshrinker, who was the only person in all of Salt Lake that I could talk to (and how I lived for Wednesdays at 3:00—it was the only time in my life where anything seemed to make any sense). I did not use the headshrinker like most people, telling him stories about my miserable feelings and such, instead, I would write stories to tell him every week. Get them in my head and tell them to him for an hour each week. (Like Anaïs Nin, except that he was getting paid to hear them.) The stories were all of a sexual nature, my favorite one about my being abducted by four men who tied me up and performed unceasing oral sex upon me, until I blacked out. He would tell me how these stories made him feel aroused. I never thought about how I was being exploited, only, somewhere, about myself being a writer and a storyteller. He must have had guilty feelings about what was going on, because one day he told me that he was quitting this line of work and going to start only doing research. Feeling betrayed, and very pissed off, I rose from my chair and gave him the evil eye, complete with the part where you spit between your fingers. He wanted to kiss and hug me goodbye, and I said "you will never touch me," threw the door open, walked down into the street and went home, where I sat in my room until Linda called. After a ten-minute conversation, she said, "Rosy, listen carefully, you have got to take your ass and put it on a bus and get out of there, now. I will come and get you if you want me to, but you have got to get the hell out of your parents' house right now."

Telling Mom and Dad that I was going to visit Linda for a two-week period, after which I would return home and get a job, was the only way they would have ever allowed me to get on that bus and leave at all. I remember seeing Geraldine, who was fourteen years old, crying, and looking at her through the bus window, I cried too, for her, mostly, because she was going to have to be the Big Sister now. She would not speak to me again until she was twenty-two years old, after having worked out her feelings of hatred and abandonment towards me, so you, dear reader, must figure out here, what would be so horrible, so hideous that it would take eight years to be able to speak of it?

After eight hours, when the bus pulled into Grand Junction, Colorado, I got off, went into the terminal, and vomited. Standing outside in the Colorado air, and taking what felt like the first free breath of my entire life . . . leaving home, this time not institution-bound, but leaving home for my own life, my own self. Back on the bus, and eight more hours later, with a hideous headache, the doors of the bus swung wide and all disembarked. There waiting for me was Chad, Linda's best friend, a cute guy with hair down past his shoulders and Linda, looking like the Mountain Queen of all the

Hippies. I was wearing false eyelashes and a sweater two sizes too small. Chad was instantaneously in love with me. Linda said, "We'll go down to the Motor Inn and use their bathroom." I was speechless at this time, it was very dark, very strange, very exhilarating.

We got to the Motor Inn and a guy came out, the night clerk, because when you went in, a buzzer summoned him, and he would come out, to see if you needed a room. This guy was the cutest guy in the world, his hair was really long and he had on a jean jacket, torn up, torn up jeans, leather moccasins and a cigarette dangling out of his mouth. Strains of Joni Mitchell poured from the room he had come out of. My God. We followed him into the room behind the desk, where he lived, and there sat two more of the most gorgeous hippie men I had ever seen and only dreamed about in my state of mind, which was the state of Utah.

After sitting down, I went immediately into what has always been this odd thing about me. When nervous, or excited, I tend to process all the shit in my head out loud. Telling every new person everything about me, wanting them to know me immediately, revealing myself too much, usually pushing them away (this is probably the real reason that I needed to go on stage). I told them all that I had just left home, escaped, and was now ready to take a lot of drugs and have sex a lot. They became quite quiet, and the night clerk stared at me, sideways. I asked him if he was Chinese, he said no. I said, I'm just trying to be "aggressive," a bit which David Steinberg had just done on TV a night before, in his crazy psychiatrist bit.

Linda was laughing, and then we went home to her apartment, which was three miles out of Georgetown proper, at the junction where two highways meet, and her apartment was underneath a rock and roll bar, called the Lift. And the bar was full of MEN. The kind of men that I yearned for at that time, dreamt about and stole fleeting glances at parts of their beings that nice girls from Utah can only imagine never having really looked at *one* at that time.

I remarked about how I was going to go down to the apartment and go to bed. Two guys said, "Do you want company?" sending me into a catatonic state of shock. Going down to my room alone, experiencing very titillated dreams of men interspliced with pictures of my little sister Geraldine screaming at me, I slept.

The sounds of rock and roll were deafening, they shook the walls, and your head would keep the beat, even if you'd not want it to; it was involuntary. It was so appropriate, in a rock and roll age, the music of rock and roll shaking walls, windows and floors of the five apartments below where young people were rocking and rolling on top of and underneath each other, and keeping the beat of the music all night long.

One of our roommates was named Randi, and she was a girl who did all the things that I was afraid to do and only fantasized about. You had to go through her room to get to the bathroom in the morning, and a lot of times there would be a different guy sleeping with her in the morning than there was the night before when you went to the bathroom. I wished all the time that I was like her, not a repressed Jewish girl with great sexual fantasies that fear would not allow to become flesh. Linda, who worked upstairs, was quite perturbed at Randi's behavior, and threw her out three days later, after her car, which all of us used, broke down. She had many places to go, so we were not too concerned.

Drucinda Ann Slocum, who had just come to town, and was living with her brother, Stretch, who had come out from Albany two years earlier, moved in. She was Catholic, and a virgin, and so she and I had many things in common and much to discuss. Dru and I continually talked about how we would meet our fantasy hippie man and Fall In Love, which was the only way we could imagine having sex with someone, they had to love you, and you them, or at least really deep Like, and Linda was the same way, we all admired girls who could just have one-night stands, but all of us knew that we couldn't be that casual about it. Two Catholic girls, one from an old Italian family, one from an old Irish family, and one from a Jewish Utah family.

Were there ever more repressed females together under one roof? I ask you. It seemed to us that Protestant girls were the ones who had it made, having a much more relaxed sexual point of view, they were the ones that at picnics could easily take off their clothes and go skinny dipping in the creek, their very blonde hair waving in the mountain breeze, wood nymphs with very little shame. We hated their guts. Whilst they would be acting such, we three girls would be divvying up the picnic food and making sure that everyone's share was equal. The soulless bitches. I really thought at that time that the fates would never smile upon me enough to ever meet any male person who would love me and care about me, whom I could have sex with, who would not just use me and then cast me aside, like all the stories your mom told you about a girl who Let Men Have Their Way. My mom was sure that this was the class of women-who-became-waitresses common story. After their sexual degradation by some male, what was left for them but to work at the minimum wage with varicose veins and hairnets hoping someday to meet just the right Trucker to carry them away to a better life in sub-suburbia? The Trucker who, like a phantom, never took them away but just talked them into having more sex out in their trucks parked in the lot, and then promising to return soon, disappeared?

But what was going on around me sexually was accepted, and I saw that the men were not just having their way with the women, and leaving, or carving notches in the bedposts. Men and women were friends there, and would laugh and talk about how they had ended up in bed together, and had a great time. This was contrary to my bringing up, and I could not believe it, that you could have sex just for fun, and not feel degraded or ashamed, but this was the first time in my life I had ever known Protestants.

I was enchanted by them, and only at a much later date realized that they were so free because they had so little culture of their own and that that is the reason that they do not understand people who do, and why they fear and loathe us, subconsciously. They actually do have a culture, I found later, having married into them, and it is about garage sales and mom and apple pie and the flag. Theirs is the dominant culture, and when I realized that, it made me feel better and better about being Jewish (because I hated myself for not being like them, for feeling like such a freak, then I realized that my self-hate was only a matter of being a minority within a majority).

Various cultures come to America and think that normal means Protestant, and try to assume that lifestyle, ironically at the same time that Protestants try to sing like black people, try to be wittily neurotic like Woody Allen's movies, read Carlos Castaneda's accounts of Mexican folklore and dress like Indians, or Italians, or Europeans. I realized that everyone is culturally fucked up in America, not just Jews. Wouldn't it be great if everyone just for one day was who they really are, and it would be OK? Then we would just enjoy our differences and stop trying to be the same? That would be nirvana to me—and it would mean many more paid Holidays.

Four days after moving in with Linda, Chad came over to our apartment with the Night Clerk from the Motor Inn. They wanted to know if Linda and me wanted to go down the road and have a beer at the Herringbone, which was a house where this old couple had turned their living room into a bar, and their backyard into a trailer court. Linda was working that night and Chad said, "Well, then do you just wanna come?" I said "I'm only nineteen, don't you have to be twenty one?" They explained that here, in Colorado, you could drink 3.2 beer when you're 18. Imagine my joy. So we crossed the creek on foot, and sidled up to the bar, where you could order frozen pizza too. My god, all of my Marlo Thomas as "That Girl" dreams were beginning to come true. Amazed and delighted at the fact that merely by going on a bus 500 miles from home, one could find beer, pizza and sexual healing, my soul began to come alive, stirring in my 130-pound body.

Drinking my very first beer, which Chad told me to add a little salt to, and being with not one, but two males, was overwhelming to me . . . they wanted to know about me, and this was the first time in my life where I was encouraged not to be a good listener, and ask the guy how He felt about everything, but that *two* males wanted to listen to me. It was glorious. So, I overprocessed, telling them everything, from how my face became paralyzed to the nuthouse. The night clerk, whose name turned out to be Bill, told me that I was the most interesting chick he had ever met, and that he was "totally blown away at how intelligent I was, since most of the other chicks he had met were stupid, shallow and petty." (Yes, he'd never met a Jewish woman.) What a compliment, to have been raised against my own subgroup, to be the Token once again, it was so comfortable to me then, to be the Example, the Exception, that I never even thought to question the insulting nature of such a statement. I also thought it was a compliment when males screamed at you from their cars then, too.

Despite the fact that they had made such statements about "chicks," they were the most gentle, sweet twenty-year-old boys in the world, they were not like the boys back home, they were so friendly, so disarming. After two beers, I was blasted, and they suggested that we go over to the Motel and listen to records. We went to Bill's "Pad," as it was called then, and he put on Joni Mitchell's "Ladies of the Canyon," which was the song of Our People, who lived there in a huge canyon full of quiet and mother nature. Bill asked me if I was still hungry, because he had some leftover Hamburger Helper and salad from dinner. I said yes, and he served it to me on a plate, with a glass of iced tea. Must you be told about how my head was spinning and my entire heart, mind and soul was trying to digest and process the fact that a man had served food to ME, that He had actually cooked himself? There was no precedent for this in my entire realm of consciousness.

I had fallen madly, passionately in love with someone who had to be home all night long, because he was a night clerk, and if he screwed up his job, he would be homeless . . . what a perfect setting for romance . . . a man, almost a captive who could not leave me, whom instead, I could leave, well it was just too highly erotic for yours truly. Sitting on the couch next to Chad, who was putting his arm around me, facing Bill, in his leather chair with a horse's head carved onto it, who began telling scary stories, campfire stories, in a small room of a motel at the bottom of a huge ring of mountains which was in Colorado, and was 500 miles from Utah, transported me away from everything that had ever threatened to consume, gnarl, destroy me. I felt Free. Chad became very excited, and said, "Bill tells the best stories, man." While I was sitting there listening, my head was throbbing and caving in, here was a man, a twenty-year-old man, telling

a typical guy-with-a-hook-for-a-hand story with bro-
cade embellishments and strings of adjectives that
heightened the horror, with dips and crescendos of
words, creating this story (which we had all heard
10,000 times anew) and I knew then that this was
the Man, my soulmate, that God himself had
planted somewhere in a small town, Security, Colorado, who had lived the exact same life as me, never
feeling safe, never feeling inside, full of fear and
self-doubt, who had survived by telling stories, and
was now right here with me. Just four days after
leaving Utah.

Chad was getting very close, moving closer,
as Bill kept on with the story that had now become
the story of a great Drunk (which he was) Irish poet
(which he was) and I started to concentrate, to send
a message to him to say, telepathically, if you do
not reach over and touch me now, Chad will, and
then you will never try to do it again, because I
know how you think, and I will go home with
Chad, because I am lonely, and I will stay with him,
and never try to touch you again. Out of nowhere,
he stopped, looked at me, and leaned over and
kissed me. Chad walked out, and we kissed more
and more and then he said, "I can't believe I did
this, to Chad, I'm so shy, I've never made a move
on a chick like that in my whole life, I can't believe
I did it, you know?" And I said, "Well, some things
maybe are just meant to be."

And some things, maybe just are, but having
sex was not one of them. Getting up, to go to the
bathroom, I spotted a copy of *The Sensual Man,* and
wondered if this was just a game, where he told me
what was just a line of shit, and after a night of wan-

ton sex, I would just be turned into a story he would tell to other guys. Coming back from the bathroom, I made it clear that we would not have sex that night, because I had forgotten to take my birth control pill that day. He said that was OK, and that he would like it if he could just wash my hair. He did wash my hair that night, massaging my scalp very slowly and gently, rinsing it, then drying it with a towel. We slept together in his bed, dressed, with our arms around each other. In the morning, his friend, Les, just walked in the room, and then stood there shocked. "Sorry," he said, closing the door. We got up and went in to talk to him.

I was so afraid that Bill would humiliate me in front of Les, and that I would have to snake out of there. He didn't though, instead, he sat by me, talking to Les, including me in the conversation, enjoying what I said, he did not become the monstrous male that Utah girls expect after exposing themselves in intimacy. Right there and then my brain had decided that my body was going to have sex with Bill. Calling him aside, I said, "I'm going to go home to Linda's, get my birth control pills and come back and have sex with you tonight." He said nervously, "Well, don't feel that you have to do that, I mean, come back, and we can talk or watch TV, or something, but that's not the only thing to come back here for, OK?" Can any man be any more sensitive than that? Actually, he told me later, that he was absolutely terrified to have sex with me, because he had just come here from LA, off a bad acid trip, and wanted only to be a hermit, to listen to Joni Mitchell records, and do crossword puzzles for a decade or so, until he was sure there would not be any flashbacks. He was afraid to get into any relationships, because he felt so shattered.

Off in my own storybook romance, though, I did return that night with my birth control pills and clean clothes, I was as ready as I would ever be, and he was in shock. Shocked that I had returned, first, and second that I had just said, "Let's do it." For a long time, Bill was between wanting me and wanting to be alone. But we did "do it" that night, and every night and day, and lunchbreak, for the next several weeks.

I was so in heaven that I did not even bother to dress at all. While he was working in the next room I just wrapped a sheet around myself, and sat waiting for him, smoking cigarette after glorious cigarette. At ten, when he closed down the motel, we would begin until six in the morning when we'd sleep until four in the afternoon, when he would get up and get ready for work, eat, and punch in at 6 P.M. We never spoke. I was still uncomfortable talking to someone I had just had sex with, and he was still uncomfortable talking to someone he lived with.

I felt the honeymoon was over one night when, as I was kissing him and the TV was on (to create a mood), he sat upright, and said, "No, stop. I've got to hear this." It was a guy talking about how people from other planets had colonized the earth. It was on Dick Cavett, and Bill considered this information to be some of the most important information he had ever heard. I was incensed, felt rejected, and hitchhiked home. By this time, everyone in the county knew about me and Bill, but

Linda was the only person who thought we would be together for the rest of our lives. She stated it aptly that night, as I was pouring out my heart to her, "Well, you bring out the weirdness in him, and he calms you down, you guys will get back together."

Neither of us were that sure of it, though, and he came over the next day and told me his now infamous . . . "I'm a ramblin' guy and I've gotta wander" speech. He told me that the way he saw it, he wanted to be a river, that rolls down the bend, and comes in contact with other streams, creeks, that flow in and away from him, and that I was one of those creeks, or streams, and that he wanted to have many more of them, not just one. Well, that no-good-for-nothing phony bastard, to have taken my young heart and squashed it under his cheap fuckin' hiking boot. "Get the fuck out," was what I remember saying.

That night, enraged, and full of hate, I went over to his house and walked up to him and started to kiss him, he placed both of his arms in the air, like he was not going to touch me, like he could withstand this great test of his male will, and then, he folded, and then he surrendered. So, I stayed a few more days, but then it happened again, he refused to incessantly rutt away his life with me, and kept foolishly insisting that there were other things to Life. He wanted to have separation with me, and I wanted to get closer and closer. You know how men are.

Well, there were other fish in the sea, and I began to want to go fishing. After doing so, I just kept getting more and more depressed, because

Bill was the Man, and why couldn't he see that, the stupid fucking bastard. Les, his friend, took me aside, and said "He's not used to this much attention, this much sex, this much togetherness, it's freaking him out." As I previously mentioned, he'd never met any Jewish women.

"Just go away for a while and he'll come back to like you, he'll work it out." So be it.

Linda had told me that they might need someone at the Silver Queen, which was the premier French restaurant in all of Colorado, where people would actually drive the snaking I-40 up from Denver to dine. Upon walking in, a huge man dressed in a chef's outfit asked, "Are you looking for work?" "Yes," I replied, "do you need a busgirl?" He said, "No, what I need in an assistant chef. Have you ever cooked before?" I said, "No." He said, "Good, you're hired." Then we went into the kitchen and he made hollandaise sauce, in about five minutes. He snarled, "Did you see that? Pay attention, cause I'm only going to show you once." Then he went and got himself a drink, came back and made chocolate mousse. Again, he asked if I had gotten that, because he did not have time to ever show me again. I became terrified, told him that I didn't think I had indeed gotten it yet. He threw a cookbook at me and said, "For Chrissakes, go home tonight and learn this."

Being from Utah, I did. One of the positive things I learned about being from Utah was to be extremely task-oriented, and disciplined, and after moving away from there, was beginning to see that other folk did not use the same applied discipline, and in fact, they were doing jobs that in Utah might take an hour, or a morning, and completing them over a two-day period. That is why the beehive is Utah's state symbol, it implies industry, getting the job done. Talking to others who grew up in Utah was very informative, because every one of them who had moved away has remarked on the same thing to me. I returned the very next day as a French chef, and B. O. Early was blown away. He started to fuck with my head. Drinking was one of his great hobbies, and browbeating his wife and all of the women who worked for him was the second, and like all men who are like that, he had a daughter whom he adored, and showered lavish praise and attention on. These are the women who, when they grow up, become like Phyllis Schlafly, the deadliest enemies of other women. Let me pause here and feel great disdain. Anyway, he would tell me to add tarragon to the simmering stock, and then go get another drink. When he returned, he would scream, "Who in the Sam Hell told you to put tarragon in there?"

Chad was a waiter there, then, and he would say, "I can't believe how that fat bastard fucks with you." Chad would always stick up for me, and tell B. O. that he himself, B. O. Early, had told me to, and that Chad had heard him say it. B. O. never argued with the males. This gave me a lot of strength, and one day I was sure I'd be able to make my point and humiliate B. O. back.

The day soon came. "B. O.," I said, "you forgot to buy English Muffins in your order yesterday." "Goddamnit, chumley" (his name for me),

"What the Sam Hell is wrong with your brain, there is a freezer full of English Muffins in there!" I had checked and checked again, everywhere, every square inch of that kitchen, and was quite sure there were no English Muffins anywhere, sure that this time it would be B. O. who would be humiliated in front of all the other employees. "No, B. O.," I said, sure of my point, "there are no muffins, because you were drunk yesterday when that delivery guy came, and you probably forgot to order the muffins, they are not here. There are no English Muffins here!!!!!" B. O. flew into one of familiar fits of rage, his drink sloshing over the rim of his glass, red rat's eyes glowering, his fat quaking and he tried to run, and he ran right past me and opened up the freezer, and there were about 400 packages of English Muffins sitting there. How had I overlooked that freezer? In my methodical checking for the muffins, I had covered every square inch of that kitchen but the place where they were. Even Chad could not help me this time. The hollandaise sauce that evening had more than a few tears mixed up in it. Nightmares kept me awake all night, I was humiliated once again, and there was no way to face my fellow workers.

In the morning, I talked Drucinda into hitting the road with me. Let's hitchhike somewhere. Drucinda was in the same attitude as me, because she was suffering from unrequited love, and so we stuck out our thumbs and fourteen hours later arrived in SLC. It was great to see my parents and siblings, it felt so safe, sleeping there in a heap on their living room floor, and when Daddy stumbled over us in the morning, he almost had a heart attack. He said he wondered how two filthy hippies had gotten into the house, during the night, and then, focusing, said to himself, "It's just Rosy and another girl." We visited all day and slept there again that night, but things were already beginning to feel too familiarly oppressive, so Dru and I decided to leave the next day, and had Mother drive us to the bus station, where we paid $3 each and rode into the next town, got off the bus and hitchhiked back to Georgetown.

We loved to hitchhike and travel. We would walk a lot of the way, and while we were walking we would sing camp songs and "Blowin' in the Wind," and Dru also loved "The Sound of Music," so we sang all of those songs, too. Dru had a beautiful voice. We would venture off the highway at times, to pick flowers to bring back and dry, or interesting stones and shells and bottle caps, which we would pack in our pockets and backpacks. The trucks and the cars whizzing by us as we were in the green wilderness would be the reminders of mankind's achievements, what mankind had wrought out of the frozen tundra, and we were womankind, viewing it, while picking bouquets of wildflowers.

Truckers would usually be the ones who would stop to pick us up, and they were the most wonderful men in the world then to us, because they were On the Road, too. When you are On the Road, all the world's laws and rules are suspended, and the only Real Thing is Speed and that's why you wave to other people in big rigs and why you stop for hitchhikers when you are driving a big truck. You acknowledge a fellow/sister traveler, acknowledge that you too are beyond the realm of the stationary world and its taboos, acknowledge that Life itself is only a long Road that you, moving extraordinarily fast and encased in futuristic metal machinery, are eating up with your eyes, and spitting out behind you. You are cutting the stationary air around you, and making it move, swirl and fly. You are the one who is in control, because you are moving, moving powerfully fast, even though you are sitting almost absolutely, and trancelike still. In a way, in this way, you are transcending the world itself.

When you are picked up, you sit in the cab of the truck with a trucker, and you look at his leathery, windworn face, and you see in it the faces of pirates, and sailors, of explorers and cowboys, of fishermen and wanderers, and every one of them is a storyteller, and every one of them asks you for your stories first, listens, and is amused when you cuss and swear and use the language of the road, and when they are satisfied, that you are indeed On the Road, and not just a dilettante, they tell you their stories, stories that mark a time before you joined them here, just to let you know that this road used to go through other, smaller, some now-dead towns that you do not know of, and you will never again pass down this road without remembering that it was here long before you were. All you can ever say is "WOW."

The truckers buy you food, drinks, let you play with their CB radios, and when they let you off, they always thank you for your company. They never try to be daddy, boss, pimp or lover, only Brother, and to me they are everything that is decent and mystical and powerful in the American Male.

Right here is where I'd like to paint this incredible picture in words about our country and how I traveled it (I mean her). I could relate some stories about old men I've met, and roadside cafes and coffee shops where I ate some incredible cheeseburgers (bought for me by a trucker), or something just the tiniest bit heartwarming. Like that bulldog-faced guy from Minnesota with the endless heartwarming stories about the heartwarming American people, and some fake town he invented in Minnesota, with Gramma's cookies and Uncle Alvin's whittlins, and with no ethnic minorities or labor unrest, yeah, some town on a lake where everybody is excruciatingly whitebread, and actually happy about it.

Then I think I'd like to write some real lyrical story about the values of the American people (which are of course battered, but still intact) or a story about riding the rigs with modern-day cowboys in trucks who still take pride in the idea of a job well done, or some kind of real beat Jack Kerouac poem which would have a lot of Mexicans in it.

But I think I'll save these stories for later on.

I'm always so envious to read those kinds of stories, by lots of writers better than me, who have taken every goddam lyrical heartwarming thing there ever will be to say about the American spirit, and left me to stand over here, as part of the jaded masses who have all but given up on the notion of heroines or renegades.

Out in America, where I was a hobo and a

gypsy, where I would stick out my thumb and Go, the most common thing I saw or experienced was that practically everyone is the same religion, and it's not mine. People who pick you up in cars love to talk about their religions, which take every wonderful thing about the awe and wonder the human species feels, and then wrings its neck, kicks it in the head, and turns it into hard-boiled dogma. I believe that Americans are a very spiritual people through being strangled by religion.

But, anyway, people who pick you up in their cars when you are hitchhiking (as opposed to Truckers who are more suited to Road Life) like to ask you if you're saved. If you politely say no, you're Jewish, you will be witness to the Jesus MoJo in all its glory. They'll start preaching to you like hell is just up the road. They think if they can convince you that they's right, then they would actually be able to believe it too. It's never the outsider they're trying to convince, it's themselves. I know 'cause I was one of them. After a while you just say yes, I am saved, 'cause I was tired of hearing about the blood of the lamb, and eating the body of Christ, and all. Whatever helps you sleep is my opinion on the subject, and that's what I like about the western world's most popular religion, it has helped put so many people to sleep, although most of them permanently and without their approval.

After you don't talk about religion, then they try to ask you if you's aware of the danger implicit in hitchhiking, then they say, for instance . . . did you hear about the two girls hitchhiking and this guy picked them up and of course he mutilates their corpses and all, then they tell a few lame jokes about black people, and they would always use that popular American term for black people. Then I would say "I don't hate black people, you know why?" and they go, "Why?" and I say "Because I've actually *known* some of them." This stuff, though tended to happen in those parts of America where people eat head cheese and wash it down with grain alcohol, so you can't really blame them.

Everyone in America (according to my generalizations) is a potential millionaire waiting for his or her big break. I was astonished lately to realize that Americans are definitely believing in and planning for the future, despite the fact that they elected Ronald Reagan twice. Over the last eight years, old America has definitely taken a turn for the right, everyone says. I don't really think it took any turns at all, most people already were pretty conservative, at least the ones in power, or how else would we have gotten to Vietnam in the first place? I don't think there are any more right wingers or any less right wingers, it's just that the Left got shot to death, and then scattered. When I was in Canada, and watched Canadian TV news, I was kind of shocked that every program was presenting two sides to every issue, and I couldn't really remember the last time I had seen that at home. All we ever get to see is the conservative against the Liberal, and the Liberal has no politics at all, anyhow. The left, or radical view, that I grew up with in the sixties is gone . . . gone from the everyday news, and views, but still very strong with women's groups. Since women are the new Left, I can understand why everyone says The Left is Dead. Our society makes the women who aren't helpers, supporters and subordinates invisible. Does anyone see them?

Conservatives are really smart people, and like P.T. Barnum, have gotten rich by never overestimating the intelligence of the American people. I think conservatives are basically assholes. If you watch them closely for a minute or two, you will be able to recognize that they are the same kids in elementary school who ate their boogers, and I bet most of them still do, too. Can't you just imagine George Bush, Pat Robertson, Reagan, Nixon, et al., hiding behind their respective school buildings sort of removed from the group, chewing on a you know what, enviously eyeing the children who could actually make friends, and then, with their weak chins aquiver, they would screw up their faces and scream, "I'm telling!" as they conjure up all the tight-lipped Protestant rage that they are capable of mustering? What we need is a Woman, a mother for President, and I'm going to run someday, and my campaign motto will be "Let's vote for Rosie, and put some new blood in the White House—every twenty-eight days."

Returning to Georgetown, I explained my absence to B. O. by saying that I had gotten very ill and had to go to the hospital in Denver. He told me that that was OK, because he had hired a new chef, a guy named Jerry, and now I was the dishwasher. At first disappointed, I became at ease when realizing that dishwasher meant working alone—and away from B. O. Early. Every time after returning from the Road, things seemed to work themselves out. Jerry had just returned from the Peace Corps in Korea, and while he worked, he would teach me Korean bird and love songs. He also talked a lot about how in the next twenty years, Japan was going to control trade in the U.S. and the world—he was a prophet in 1972. When he was drunk, his singing would become louder and louder until it disturbed the customers, but being as they were Turkeys (our name for tourists) they would want to come back into the kitchen to hear the quaint little songs of the quaint little townspeople. This made B. O.'s restaurant even more popular, and he encouraged it.

Around this time, Mrs. Early, drunk and driving, wrapped her car around a telephone pole and died immediately. Mr. Early drank even more after that and became even more brutal, so I had to tender my resignation. Dru and I once again hit the road. We went to San Francisco this time. When we came back, we decided to stop in SLC, and Dru became very homesick for her own family in Albany, so we decided to go there next. Stopping home in Georgetown first, Bill was not all that happy to see me, as all we ever did by now was fight and try to hurt each other. Before I left, I took all of my underwear and put them in his kitchen sink, soaked them with water and left. We got to Albany, and now all I could think of was going to New York City. I knew that that was where *Mad* magazine was, my all time favorite literature, and I wanted to see it. New York City had always beckoned me when I was a kid in SLC, because I knew that that was where all the Jews were, and I wanted to see other Jews so badly my whole life. Sometimes, from Philadelphia on, we would get rides from Jewish guys, and it would be exciting, so heavenly. Jews Jews everywhere and not a drop to drink.

Somehow, I'd gotten very very sick before we got to go into the city. Dru took me to a hospital on Long Island where they told me I had mononucleosis and needed to go home immediately. I called Bill. Telling him to send me the money to fly home was not the easiest thing in the world to do. He borrowed it from his parents and sent it to me, and we flew home. Linda and Chad picked us up at the airport and drove us back to Georgetown. They took me to Bill's house and he was worried about me. He took me in and put me to bed, and took care of me. We made love, even though I had a temperature of 104. I said to him, "I have mono. Maybe we shouldn't do this." He said, "Well, that's OK, I just won't kiss you then." That's how we were, madly in love, but hating each other the whole time. He took me to the hospital the next day, and after two days there I contracted hepatitis also.

Coming home, he let me stay at his apartment, and he slept in the other room. A day or two later, Chad's cousin Mary Beth came to visit. She and Bill had some mystery between them, since she and Bill and Chad had grown up together in Colorado Springs. Originally, Bill came to Georgetown because Chad's brother-in-law Steve was the manager of the Motor Inn, and needed a night clerk. Bill, fresh from being a reporter and record critic on the Colorado Springs *Sun* newspaper, had dropped acid for the first time and decided to go to live in

LA. After a miserable six months there, he returned home and tried to get reinstated in his old job. The paper had been sold then, though, and new people had replaced him. Every day, at his mother's urging, he would get up and go out to look for a job. Or so his mother thought. What he really did was go drive to a park and sleep in his car. So, when Chad called with the job, he readily went, thinking that he would be able to put himself back together after a real bad acid trip.

Everyone came to Georgetown that way, because they knew someone else there, because it was in the mountains, and the mountains were unspoiled, hidden and presented a way for you to remake yourself, away from what had sent you here. There were so many writers and musicians and sculptors and painters and clothing designers there, who had been bank clerks or rich kids or abused children, or ex-wives, or dispossessed fathers, so many entrepreneurs who had previously been clerks, so many lonely people, so many outcasts, so many storytellers who were now remaking themselves, and remaking society because of that. We had all found a haven from the city "shit," which was Vietnam, Nixon, upheaval and the "straights," which was what we called the establishment. We had all found a place to hibernate, to mend our wounds, our separateness.

The Motor Inn was one of the only places around that had running water, and everyone would gather there or at Chad's to bathe, and bath night is the night that Linda and me and Dru would charge everyone $4 and cook a community spaghetti dinner. We'd all smoke pot and eat, then Bill

would insist everyone listen to his comedy albums
and Joni Mitchell. It was so wonderful then.

Georgetown at that time was a curious mix of the
real and the fantastic; both worlds could merge and
intermingle with ease if they wanted to. One night
Bill and I were up late, absorbed in yet another
giant crossword puzzle, when we got our first taste
of the easy supernatural sensuality that the times
and the mountains could create.

We had both heard the tale, told by many with
deadly seriousness, of the ghost train. Georgetown
had been a silver mining giant in the last century,
and had been the hub of the many narrow gauge
trains that made their way down from other mining
communities with their loads of ore. The legend
said that on certain nights, around 2 A M , one of
the trains would pull into 1970s Georgetown right
on the same schedule it had adhered to in the
1890s. The trains, and their tracks, and all attend-
ant hardware, had of course been gone many years.
Only the graded beds remained now, the province
of four-wheel drive vehicles. We loved the romance of the tale but had never really given it too
much serious thought. But on this night, at 2 A.M.,
in the midst of the *Sunday New York Times* crossword puzzle, 24 down (a nine-letter word for *capri-
cious*), we felt the fabric tear between our world and
all worlds before it. Out of the night came the
sound of a chugging, puffing behemoth, churning
carefully down from the pass, running along behind the motel, and parking a block away. One of
my biggest regrets to this day is that Bill and I were

both too afraid to look out the window to see if the train really was there.

We had our reasons. Bill's boss had heard the trains many times before over the years, and when we had asked him if he had ever looked out of the window, his eyes would widen and he would say, "Of course not. If I saw it, I'd have to board it out of curiosity and I would cease to exist." That had been good enough for us. We just sat and listened to the engines for a moment more, until they faded into the night and back to the time from which they had come.

The early seventies had their share of the unusual too, but of a more earthbound variety. The first chinks in our perfect world begin to appear then; when the belief that we were all brothers and sisters with the same mind evaporated into cold reality. No more could one count on knowing where the group soul was at. It had begun to splinter and break and fragment into many factions now; some taking to caves in the hills to embrace Mescalito; others returning to their New England catholic homes; still others beginning to embrace what would become the yuppie mentality of the eighties.

However, none of our group struck more fear into me than the new disciples of the Guru Mahara Ji, a tubby precursor to Jabba the Hut, who laid claim to being the son of God. His followers had to renounce all that was material in their world, and as long as they wouldn't be needing the wealth anymore, the Guru was more than happy to take it. Oh, and as long as they were at it, would they mind too terribly much not having any social or physical contact with their "old" families and friends?

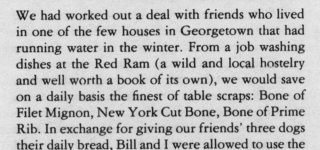

We had worked out a deal with friends who lived in one of the few houses in Georgetown that had running water in the winter. From a job washing dishes at the Red Ram (a wild and local hostelry and well worth a book of its own), we would save on a daily basis the finest of table scraps: Bone of Filet Mignon, New York Cut Bone, Bone of Prime Rib. In exchange for giving our friends' three dogs their daily bread, Bill and I were allowed to use the bathtub on Tuesday nights. Since our log cabin had only an outhouse and a pump outside, the chance for a warm, running indoor bath was a pleasure not to be taken lightly.

It was on one of these bath nights, while Bill soaked in the tub and I sat on the stool waiting my turn, that there came from within the walls the highest-pitched moaning and caterwauling that I had ever heard. At first we thought it was yet another ghost, but on closer listening we could tell it was a man and a woman sobbing hysterically in one of the other rooms. We knew then who it was. One of the young newlywed couples in our extended family had "gone over" to the good Guru only days before; I guess the gnashing of teeth was just part of the "bliss" that the Mahara Ji promised.

Ashamed for ourselves, and for them, Bill got out of the tub, dried off and we went into the night, shaking our heads and wondering what would become of all of us. We never had bath night again after that; the family was just too far disseminated under the same roof now. But spring was coming and soon more bathtubs would become available as the ground gave up its deep frost. And new bath-tubs meant meeting new people.

Georgetown had the singular and particular knack of attracting only the most unusual and inter-esting characters that America had to offer: My friend, Linda, who taught me the science of herb-gathering gleaned from the knowledge that being a seventh-generation mountain girl brings; Andy, the Red Ram cook, whose claim to fame was con-fronting a customer who had complained about the food. Totally naked, save for a bloodied apron and a meat cleaver, Andy sat down at the man's table and inquired as to what the problem was. There was none, it turned out. And seventy-year-old Henry Anderson, who to this day owns and man-ages the same general store that has been in his fam-ily for over a hundred years.

And there were others. All kinds of people from all kinds of places and all kinds of circum-stances who had come to Georgetown to be with all kinds of their own: The Outsiders.

And what fun we could make together! I re-member washing dishes one hot July afternoon and hearing the sound of ragtime piano fill up the park-ing lot outside the restaurant. All of the waitresses and cooks begin running into the lot, where I could hear their laughter. I rushed outdoors and to my delight saw four very drunk Georgetowners in a pick-up truck. Set up in the bed was an old upright piano, skillfully played by a local ragtime musician who sat bare-chested on the wall of the bed, suck-ing on a cigar. Next to the piano was a pony keg, from which the brew spilled freely for all of us. As we sipped the suds in the hot mountain air and listened to Scott Joplin music, the customers inside began to notice no staff was in the restaurant. They must have thought us quite mad as we stumbled giggling back into the restaurant, joshing and pushing each other, the smell of beer on all of our breaths.

Professional drinking, however, was reserved for the volunteer fire department, made up of the finest young men that Georgetown could offer. Every Fourth of July it was the fire department's duty to safely oversee the fireworks display from the side of nearby Leavenworth mountain. The town would spend the day in drunken and stoned anticipation, waiting for the fall of darkness which would signal the assault. Scores of residents would gleefully yell "Incoming!" and run for cover as errant fireworks would drop into the town, exploding in people's yards and looking very much like the end credits for *Apocalypse Now*. Somehow nobody ever got hurt, and what random fires did erupt were quickly snuffed by the ever-vigilant squad of pyrotechnicians.

The department's finest moment, however, was the glorious day that the new fire engine arrived from Denver by train. The celebration began at the firehouse as soon as the truck arrived, and people admired it while keg after keg of brew was extinguished by the lusty troops. Eventually someone noticed that the keys were in the truck and within moments, townsfolk in their quiet mountain homes were awakened rudely by a siren just outside their window. In an effort to show all of the people the new truck, the fire department was obliging by going door to door and firing the truck up in all of its glory. I remember looking out of the Motor Inn window at the commotion and seeing twenty or twenty-five drunken young men hanging to the truck by every available nozzle, hook, ladder rung and hose, yelling wildly into the mountain night as they basked in the red glow of the revolving lights. They don't fight fires like that anymore.

Soon, though, we began to hear about this guy, John Denver, who would sing all these stupid songs about the mountains, and we started to notice all these people starting to come, the same people that we now call yuppies, yes, they have always been amongst us, we called them "city freaks," and the old houses and cabins were not good enough for them, they came with a Vision of Condos, and dams and tourist attractions. They had a series of town meetings where they explained to all of us "quaint" hillbilly folks that they were going to build condos that would be keeping the environment intact, and bringing more tourist dollars, therefore, higher pay to us and our town. We did not trust them, and Dru stood up in the town meeting and said, "I will lay my body down in front of your bulldozers, and stop you any way I can." We all cheered, all of us were sure that the old would be able to stop the new, and that we could keep our town small and untouched. We did succeed in postponing it for a while. We knew however, all of us, that something was going to happen. That's why I still hate that fucking John Denver.

CHAPTER
13

Exhilarating, exciting and sharp, at first the feeling is pleasant. This is the beginning of the end of a long wait, soon all the prayers and hopes that have been with you every moment will be over. An hour or two will pass in quick, metered time divided by the tightenings and relaxations in your belly.

I was a girl just a short time ago and I dreamed of this so many times, my own child, my own family, I will be a mother. I think of my own mother and imagine her fear. She was seventeen years old when I was born, she tells me of the pain and of the drugs and the doctors who pulled me from her with instruments that made my head misshapen. I think of my husband as my labor coach, and what a wonderful father he will be. My own father—I wonder how he looked when he was young and stood waiting outside for my mother to give birth alone in a hospital room.

Pains get closer and closer together and last longer, get harder in intensity. Breathe, my husband tells me, do your level-one breathing. I am dilated to seven my doctor tells me after a digital examination. It won't be long now. I have only one minute between my pains now it is so hard to keep on top of them. My husband is telling me to concentrate concentrate, breathe in out breathe in out stay on top of them he is squeezing my hand and shouting to me from so far away, dressed in white, barking out at me trying to control my body with his words, and all there is is pain, pain that makes me want to run to run fast and escape it and I think of the Bible that tells me this will be my fate, to bring forth children in agony and I think of Eve the first woman to give birth and how did she cope with this hideous pain that no one had ever before experienced. And my teeth felt as if the nerves were exposed and they were raw and I begged for a wash cloth to bite on to keep from grinding them and the doctor and my husband were calling to me and shouting, but I was on vacation from reality and my line was busy. What is this thing what is this thing how have women survived this? How could women have done this terrible thing alone and over and over?

I can feel the full weight of the body inside mine as it struggles to escape. It is heaving and throwing itself violently against my organs and my skin and my nerves. It is screaming to get out and I am afraid it is a monster, a terrible vicious thing that will destroy me with its strength. I am screaming for it to get out of me as if I am conducting an exorcism and my brain, I can see my brain crumbling like blue cheese, pieces falling out and falling off. And I hate the thing inside me that is killing me and I hate my mother because she did not warn me and I hate my husband and all men who make women pregnant.

I am going to die I am going to die, and I start screaming. My husband grabs my legs and holds them apart while the doctor sticks his fist into me again and again, measuring my uterus, violating and hurting me. Don't push yet he is saying and

I push and push and push, not yet not yet he screams, and my husband panics and says *stop!* in a big man's voice that my heart and mind and body swear not to obey.

The doctor says he can see hair, and I am imagining him dead and bloody and slumped in the corner next to my husband; and myself with bloody fangs running from the room a she wolf and I will howl at the moon for the rest of my life, there's no coming back, this torture is mind boggling. I think of the soldiers in prison camps with drops of water falling on their heads and their toenails on fire and I laugh and I laugh at their cowardice and intolerance for pain. Nothing nothing will ever be as terrifying and grotesque as this. And then I feel a pressure that begins in my lower back and it reminds me of rice paper, tearing rice paper, so swift and easy and it comes apart. It's a girl they say and my husband says oh honey it's a girl. And she is screaming and I think of her terror, she has been squeezed alive for eight and one half hours and her body has been forced through a passage tight around her head, a passage of human flesh and bone and blood blood blood. And I take her into my arms while the doctor and my husband marvel at the meaning in all of this, and I hold her, knowing that she is terrified of my body and I am torn and terrified from her body and the agony and power of motherhood now is clear to me.

Now I know why mothers love their children—because we have been one-in-hell together. Now it is all over, and I can see the monster and she can feel the machine of my grinding, twisting body, now giving comfort, as I give her my breast and think of a poem:

I am a woman giving birth to myself.

CHAPTER 14

Recipe Cards

Recipe for ChiliMac
Get 1lb. of hamburger, cook it, drain it
Cook a package of noodles, macaroni
   noodles are best
Drain
Add 2 cans of tomato paste, one can of
   water, garlic salt, onions
Mix it all up
Put into a cake pan, preferably one with
   black and brown stains on the bottom
Cook it
Put on some grated cheddar cheese
Serve with Cokes, maybe a green salad with
   Italian dressing
Eat it

Boil some Kosher frankfurters in hot water
Get some hot dog buns
Put mustard and ketchup on the table
and a knife
Put a package of onion-flavored potato chips

on the table, too
Maybe some relish
Cook some ears of corn, put them on a
platter on the table
Take the hot dogs out of the water, put
them on the table
Put the stuff on the buns, add hot dog, eat
Serve with Cokes

Put a chicken in oven
Clean first
Put some salt and pepper on it
Put some garlic salt on it, too
Cook it
Put it on the table
Cook some corn muffins
Make some bean salad, 3 kinds of beans,
then put on Italian dressing
Marinate it for ten hours before you read
this

The hardest part about being an artist, I've found,
is having talent. You really cannot create unless
you are creative. I've got the urge though, it's this
little person inside trying to get out and do neat
things like make statements and lots of bold stuff:

*(Two Poems I Found that I'd Written
on the Back of Recipes)*

*I want to be like Lenny Bruce
an iconoclast straight and true*

*But I don't know what's hypocritical, even
    though I am a Jew,*

*I wanna be like Gertrude Stein, a cubist I have
read but I don't understand an inch of what the
    hell she said.*

*I wanna write poetry or a novel that would
sell—but I can't think of what to say or how to
    say it well.*

*I want to be like Germaine Greer, a speaker for
    my sex
but male and female to me are equal nervous
    wrecks.*

*The hardest part of being an artist I have found
        is trying to strike a balance
        Between the pure desire to create and having
        only meager talents.*

1977

*I live with three small and stocky people
Sometimes we have ice cream and cookies for
    breakfast.
Then the very next we have whole wheat bran
    pancakes, sliced fruit and yogurt.
We eat Big Macs at McDonalds and then go
    down the street to
Wendy's for the fries 'cause they're softer and
    greasier.*

The next day though we'll have a vegetable pie
  with whole wheat bread.
They tell me to quit smoking and I sneak
  downstairs or say I will tomorrow.
They tell me not to bite my nails.
They tell me to turn down the stereo so they can
  talk.
They'll ask about the stars so we go to the library
  and buy a telescope.
They'll ask about cowboys so we go camping and
  ride a horse.
They hate all my rock and roll records, and like
  classical.
"It reminds me of birds," Jess says.
I like to pick up bugs in the park.
"Put it down, mother," they say, disgusted.

CHAPTER

15

For all of you "house-wives" out there, which of course is a term I employ that means anybody who has ever had to clean up somebody else's shit and not been paid for it: Part of the reason that women are so confused these days is due to the horrid grotesque "women's magazines" and the type of mind-numbing bullshit they pour out on us month after hideous month. I just know they're a political conspiracy to keep women off base so we won't demand the arms race stopped and the money it uses be spent more productively. I used to read all of these shitty mags all the time when my boring life made me feel the urge to search for exciting recipes and crafts, and tips from some bitch about organizing my closet space, or worse, from a guy telling women how to keep house . . . as if we have not become experts at it from the last 5000 years of being forced to do it. When I should have been organizing other neighborhood women and storming every government office and agency and forcing them all to anoint me as your Queen, so I can clean up this world, straighten it, and organize it as only the Queen of the Housewives can do.

The thing I hate about these mags is one month they tell you to do one thing and then the next month they tell you to do just the opposite. Once, I kept a log, and it went something like this . . .

January:

- Don't drink, don't smoke, don't overeat—*Family Circle*
- Don't deprive yourself of pleasure, everything in moderation—*Family Circle*
- Are you a hedonist?—*Cosmo*

February:

- Don't overprotect your kids—*Ladies Home Journal*
- Mothers who have abandoned their kids for a career—*Family Circle*
- Women who give up their careers because they find it more fulfilling to stay home with their kids—*Redbook*
- How women need to work to supplement the family income—*Ms.*

March:

- Don't fear success—*Working Woman*
- Women who are too successful and can't find husbands—*Redbook*
- Are men intimidated by successful women?—*Redbook*
- Dress for success—*Redbook*
- How today's modern man prefers a successful woman who has her own career—*Cosmo*

April:

- How job related stress is killing more and more women—*Ladies Home Journal*
- Are women losing touch with their role as nurturers?—*Family Circle*
- How housewives are out of touch with the real world—*Savvy*

May:

- Women are moving up the corporate ladder

    —*Ladies Home Journal*
- Is the Rat Race killing us all?—*Woman's Day*

June:

- Accept those things that you cannot change, change those you can—*Ladies Home Journal*
- Don't accept things at Face Value

    —*Ladies Home Journal*

July:

- Don't cower, but don't overpower—*Savvy*
- Don't stop growing, don't drive yourself too hard, be all that you can be—*Working Woman*
- Don't overdo it—*Redbook*

August:

- Be honest, be open, stand up and be counted—*Ms.*
- Don't be so sensitive—*Cosmo*

September:

- Don't compromise your principles, listen to other people's advice—*Family Circle*
- If you can't beat 'em, join 'em—*Cosmo*

October:

- Are religious women the best lovers?
  —*Redbook*
- Women with fundamentalist beliefs stay in battering situations longer—*Ms.*

November:

- Weigh the question logically in a mathematical formation—*Savvy*
- Why most girls flunk math—*Redbook*

December:

- The joys of home birth—*Family Circle*
- Doctors say . . . the safety of hospital birth—*Woman's Day*
- Your risk of developing a staph infection in a hospital—*Better Homes*

Christ, no wonder we're all going nuts.

16

How to Lose Weight

1. Tell everybody you're going to go on a diet.

2. Lose the first ten really easily, almost without effort.

3. Tell everybody that you lost it.

4. Pay 600 hard-earned dollars to some "program where all the employees are extremely thin, and have long, manicured fingernails."

5. Go on Weight Watchers . . . and think about food every waking second.

6. Join a program where the food is included in little freeze-dried packets.

7. Exercise strenuously every day.

8. Look covetously at other women, preferably ones wearing mini skirts, patterned stockings and high heels, with long, manicured fingernails.

9. Really believe it and wait until other people notice that you have lost weight, and tell you that you look great.

10. After you have lost about half of the weight you want to lose, start worrying about being rejected for other reasons besides being fat.

11. Keep smoking.

12. Think that getting thin will really change everything.

13. Start looking at people who are fatter than you with a mixture of contempt and pity.

14. Start buying lingerie.

15. When with the opposite sex, start acting coy.

16. Notice that sales clerks, bag boys, and almost everyone who is underemployed are more courteous.

17. Get a little depressed over the above things and think, god, people really do judge a book by its cover.

18. Start to judge a book by its cover.

19. Start reading *Vogue.*

20. Apply makeup, even when you don't have to.

21. Start thinking about things you'll do when you're thin.

22. Have three weeks where you only lose a pound.

23. Think, just this once is OK, I'll make up for it tomorrow.

24. I can't beat myself up for falling off, I just need to start again tomorrow.

25. Beat yourself up about it.

26. Gain three pounds.

27. Starve two whole days.

28. Lose one pound.

29. Hate yourself.

30. Hate your friends who eat like hogs and are reed thin.

How to Gain It Back

1. Tell everybody that you gained a few back.
2. Gain the first ten really easily.
3. Tell everybody that you did.
4. Start noticing that hardly anyone you remember from your program is there anymore.
5. Start thinking about food every second, and how bland it tastes.
6. Think people who exercise a lot are really boring.
7. Start listening to what women in mini skirts actually say.
8. Shop for your clothes in specialty shops . . . notice how they really have too many flowers and too many sequins.
9. Look at the pictures in "Big Beautiful Woman."
10. Stop smoking.
11. Think that getting thin won't change anything.
12. Start looking at people who are fatter than you as people who are fun to hang out with.
13. Start buying sweat suits, for everyday wear.
14. When with the opposite sex, listen to what blowhards they are.
15. Get really angry over the above and think, god, people really do judge a book by its cover.
16. Start to judge all thin people as shallow, self-obsessed folk who never even READ anymore (you won't be far from the truth).
17. Realize that models in *Vogue,* etc., are just

as consumed by food as you are, but they're consumed and deprived, too.

18. Eat, bubele, you should eat.

19. Invite your fat friends and relatives over for a nice party, or dinner, and admit how much you've missed them, and how funny, warm, witty and dishy they all are . . . notice that one of them only eats the salad.

20. Wait three months, begin again, weighing, of course, twenty pounds more than you used to.

21. Schedule a manicure.

CHAPTER
17

There was a time when I was the Queen of the Barefoot and Pregnant. I would wait all day until Bill would come home, feeling excited about being able to speak to another adult, to exercise my brain. Bill was usually too tired, though, and could only handle watching TV and drinking beer, and somewhere in that time, I just slipped away, so far way inside myself, so far down in, that it was becoming harder and harder to even come out at all. I would try to talk to the other mothers in our building, but I was very uncomfortable, and would usually just sit staring and smiling, empty, listening to them talk about household chores and fighting with their husbands and things their kids had learned, and sometimes, the same things came out of me, but I was aping them. I just wanted to be with someone, to feel some connection. And always after the fourth or fifth time I would visit with them, I would say that I wanted to be a writer and I wanted to be a poet, and then I would tell some ideas I had for a book or a story, and these other women would look at me, like there was something wrong with me for wanting that, for saying that, for thinking about anything besides kids and dinner and husbands.

I felt there was something terribly wrong with me, too. I wasn't a good mother because good mothers were happy mothers and good wives were happy wives, and to say anything that was irrelevant to these things was quite heretical. I turned on the radio once and there was a talk show, and I just became hooked on it, absolutely hooked, on this one host/dj whose name was Alan Berg. When religious people would call in, to tell him to read the Bible . . . he would say "Why should I? I don't believe in God, anyway, it's just a book written by some guy and it's a fairy tale, OK?" Then the religious persons would avalanche call and call him everything from a commie bastard to a Satan worshipper and mostly they would, at least two or three times a day, call him a dirty Jew. He would let them say it, and then he would say, "You are a very sick, twisted, hateful person, you Nazi bastard." And here it was, the thing I actually needed, some nice brain stimulation, when the kids went down for naps, I would, for the two hours while I cleaned or washed or sewed or cooked, listen to this, this Alan Berg and say to him over and over "You tell 'em, Alan," or "You're wrong, Alan."

One day I called in, it had been three months since I had started listening and I sat down and wrote a funny little bit that I could call in and read to him.

I called, and waited, and then he said "You're on the air" . . . "Hello, Alan I really like your show," I stumbled. "What do you wanna say?" he asked, impatiently. I read the thing, and while I read it, I actually peed my pants, because I was so scared, and so rusty, so afraid. He said, "That's very funny, you make a very good point there. Please call in again, I enjoyed talking to you."

I hung up the phone and started to cry, and it went on and on and on, lots of tears. Someday,

I thought, I'll tell that old Alan Berg how much that day meant to me, and how much I'll remember it forever. Could he tell how much I needed to hear that from my quaking voice? Could he tell when someone was on the edge, when someone had lost everything and was so far down, that they would actually call up an afternoon talk show, with a pre-pared statement, and read it with a shaky voice? I think he did know, and he really did care, really did care about all the lonely ones, the wronged ones, the fucked up ones, yes, I do think he did. I always credit that day with being the first day on my way back to myself. The other glorious thing about him was that, for me, he was the first Jewish person I ever heard that dared to fight back besides my Bobbe, which was new to a Jewish girl from SLC who was raised to "not tell anyone, or they wouldn't play with you anymore, not tell anyone because they would barrage you with a wave of hate that would take you off-balance for at least a few days." But you had to tell them, because you wanted them to know who you were, because that's what friends do, and this IS who you were, but after enough times, you would stop telling, because well, you did want to have friends, even though you knew that this meant they were not really friends. So Alan Berg was the first Jewish person I had ever heard who fought back, kind of like my grand-mother, kind of like you should, no matter who you are, against communism or fascism, or whatever it is we're calling it now.

When Bill came home, I told him, I was so ex-cited to tell him and he acted like all the neighbor ladies acted, like what was the matter with him . . .

did I indeed need to be so selfish to be so heretical as to suggest that I needed something other than HIM and the kids in my life to make me happy? At first Bill always acted that way, from my calling up talk shows to my wanting to go to work part time, to my needing to talk to my sisters, to my needing to go out alone, to my needing to call a radio show, to my needing to write. So, I been there, honey.

One day while he was at work, and the guys at the Post Office had the talk show on and I called in again, and everyone heard it, and Bill said, "I think this is my wife" and he called to ask and I said yes, and he said that all the guys had enjoyed what I had to say and thought I was a regular celebrity down there at the Terminal Annex. After that, he was better.

Now there was something to talk to everyone about, to the neighbor ladies, I'd say, I gotta go listen to Alan Berg, 'cause I call in there all the time, and then I became a minor celebrity in the building, and somehow close to that magic of show business, where everything you say is taken a little more seriously now, because you've been on the radio. Someday, I thought, after a while, I'll write Alan Berg a letter and let him know how much he meant to me, and what he did for me. I almost had the chance once, sitting in a coffee shop, two seats down from him, awestruck, sweating, almost ready to say it, he looked at me, and I at him, I was thin then, and he wanted to talk to me, maybe to flirt, but I chickened out.

And then he was dead. Shot dead as he walked from his car into his apartment. Killed by the Aryan

Brotherhood, assassinated for being a Jew with a Big Mouth, for fighting back to KKKers and Nazi-Americans, for being like Lenny was, too real, too truthful, too opinionated and too Jewish and for being too Brave in the Land of the Brave, for being too free in this Home of the Free. His was a voice that inspired me to develop one, and I never got to thank him . . . till now.

CHAPTER
18

I think I was about four years old when I first saw on Ed Sullivan what I thought was a prophet of the air waves. It was a stand-up comic, and I watched him, transfixed, asking family members when it would again be Sunday. My dad loved comedy about as much as anyone ever has, and whenever the comedian would appear on Ed Sullivan, he would shout for all of us kids, but most for me . . . "Comedian! Comedian!," the siren call of the Barr family.

I watched it as a cultist, as the word of god incarnate. It was this wonderful thing that was somehow about language, and also somehow about politics, and somehow about rebellion, and resistance and anarchy. It was sad, angry, misogynistic, defiant, misogynistic, titillating, almost obscene, and misogynistic.

It was some Jewish thing, I thought then, something that Jews really owned and knew about and did better than almost anyone else. It was the Midrash, it was about connection, and the symbolic murder of the status quo, and the blurring of what is sacred and what is profane . . . a place on earth where Jews are not threatening to non-Jews and people in Utah . . . a little stage of a promised land like an island in a sea of fear. A place where a Jew can speak as a Jew, as stranger in a strange land, as a part of a group that defined itself in its own view and with its words, in a manner that seemed to heal (instead of wound). It was a vortex place where you could go and pull the rest of the world in with you, a place, like poetry where you change the way you hear, and feel and see.

Later, I would think of it as a super-political act, the power of creating a new point of view. Almost like some highly guarded night thing, that has always existed somewhere in the dark ages and after you did it, you rode away before they could hang, catch or burn you. Thoughts like phantoms, thoughts like vampires, prowling the night in search of others, others who know the joke, too. And, seeing through the ones who feel no magic, but look upon it as a way to get laid, high or loved, like it's a fix. These are always the people you hear talking about Lenny Bruce's rough language.

CHAPTER
19

Lenny Bruce was perceived in the late part of the sixties as the future. The future that meant that the old way is dead, and passing. So he, like all people who remind other people of the future, have to either die, or be invalidated while they are alive, and then after, when they are dead, people can start worshipping them as a martyr, or great teacher, and pretend to themselves that if their heroes ever came back, in this time and age, they would listen, they would agree, they would be so fuckin' hip. They are so fucking hip they are busy censoring, invalidating, and fucking with the writers, artists, poets, that belong to them during their own lifetimes. It was no accident that Lenny had chosen comedy. It is the last "free speech" art form and, like my father said, it is mightier than the pen *and* the sword.

For years I thought it wasn't worthy of me, though I adored watching others do it. I aspired to be Gertrude Stein, or Dylan Thomas, or some poetess tragically and forlornly trying to scrape some piece of misery off the sole of my soul and write some touching little fat girl shit about it. I thought fat girls had to write poetry until at a teenaged time I heard Lord Buckley, and Lenny Bruce, and understood the jazz of words alone, that had a rhythm and a beat and a sensuous movement that you could get lost in. It is a place, perhaps the only place where a woman can speak as a woman, as a stranger in a strange land, as part of a group that defined itself in its own view, and with its own words, in a manner that seemed to heal, instead of wound. It feels like combat against the literary bombardment, that came, almost without exception, from male authors . . . how we women stink, our fat removes our sexuality, how we are pushy and voracious and intrinsically evil and lost without souls, and conniving and castrating and overpowering, in need of control, and begging for degradation, and what excited me, finally, was the thought of a woman, any woman, standing up and saying NO . . . a huge cosmic "NO" and the first time I went on stage, I felt *myself* say it, and I felt chilled and free and redeemed.

CHAPTER
20

There came a time in my life that I, thinking myself a writer, walked into a place called Woman to Woman Bookstore on Colfax Street in Denver, Colorado, it was in the beginning of the 1980s. I thought I would find books by women writers, and I was looking specifically for books about women writers by women writers. It had just dawned on me that I was a woman and a writer, and each and both of these words were huge masses of veins and hair to me, all tangled together, needing to be sorted, cleaned, defined. There was a couch in the back, next to a tea machine, and everything was funky, old, musty. I thought it was really wonderful to have a couch and a tea machine in the back of a bookstore, and I thought it was really wonderful to have a woman's bookstore. I was a feminist then, happy about being given little couches in little cramped bookstores on big city streets in my life in Denver, Colorado, in 1980.

There was a sign on the coffee table in front of the couch that said this is a safe place for women. Respect it. I was a feminist then and so I was very happy about a little paper on a table in front of a musty old couch in the back of a cramped and cinderblocked bookstore for women on a big city street in a city like Denver, Colorado. I picked up several books by women writers and turning back, walked to the couch and began to read. I read sentences by all my favorite authors, I read paragraphs about all my favorite authors, I read pieces of great literature and I nodded my head when something struck home. I was a feminist then, a woman who takes herself seriously, a writer who believed that she was living in the greatest century that ever was, a part of a movement (although not at its vanguard), a movement of women that was about equal rights with men, about peace and nonviolence, but mostly about dignity and self-respect, and tossing aside hurtful traditions that are about gender and roles. About a constitutional amendment called ERA.

God, I was so very fulfilled. I had three healthy, beautiful children, a husband who loved me (and shared housework), sisters and friends, and I was thin, dark, fit, working towards a career as a buyer in the clothing industry. I was for the ERA, I had raised consciousness, I had a nice suburban home, and a subscription to *Ms.* magazine. I was working one night a month with the Committee of Concern for Soviet Jewry, writing letters, speaking, I had come up from poverty and despair and all that was behind me, it was a wonderful day for me, that day, in that bookstore on Colfax Street, as I sat in that safe space for women on the couch in the back, by a tea machine.

When I got up, I turned to look out the back window, and I noticed a staircase, going down, a staircase that went down into a basement. I asked about that staircase, what was down there. The woman said, this bookstore is run by a collective, we have meetings down there. Can anyone go I asked, yes she said. I felt elated, excited, I can go to meetings on Tuesdays I thought, noticing the leaflets, flyers, pamphlets, and maybe I will be able to write for them.

I went down the stairs and into the basement. There were many couches down there, and I thought of them filled with women like me, women who had Things To Say and wanted to write, I felt my unbirthed baby poems kick in my belly, I was ecstatic, I could belong, finally, to something. This basement was beautiful to me, all cinderblocks and wood, stone, cold, dark, with the smell of mothballs and shit, it was beautiful because it would be full of women who knew about the ERA (not like in the suburbs, where women only talked about babies and husbands and recipes and television and shopping and gossiping about other neighbors). This place would make me a writer.

Sisterhood is powerful, I thought, and dragged back a tear, for I was ever so grateful, so grateful to be living in the 1980s, in Denver, Colorado, and to have found a woman's bookstore, and a safe place to sit, and free tea, the feminine mystique and other women who were also concerned about the passage of the ERA. I got in my car, drove home, did my housework, and made dinner, told my husband, told my sisters, wrote a poem about possibilities and slept in my bed that night, strong and proud to be a woman, wife, mother, sister, writer, salesperson, so proud to be equal. Tuesday came, I had fixed everything for dinner, I had been to my part-time job, I was ready now to go from wife-mother-career woman to Writer with Something To Say. My sister Geraldine and I were in the car, driving to the collective meeting at the bookstore. We parked, we walked in. I was wearing a purple jumpsuit, high heeled shoes, and lots of makeup, I forget what my sister was wearing.

We descended into the underworld. Descending each stair carefully in my six-inch spike heels, clicking hard on the bare cement, I went down down down like Kore descending into hell: I had left my mother, Demeter, above the ground and now I was going to belong to the underworld. What I saw down in that basement, what I heard, what I spoke, became a painting that I see often in my dreams, and in my head when I'm staring into space. I saw women who were thousands of years old, the light from their eyes pierced me, I felt my brain splitting apart, I felt myself shed skin, I felt myself begin to spin and spiral out and up and away. I had no body, only a memory like a very dim light, the memory of something that hasn't happened yet.

There was that smell, there was almost no light. When my eyes became focused, I saw dozens of women, women like women I had never seen before, women who huddled in the basements of bookstores, we listened, they were talking. One was a very fat black woman with a babushka on her head. They looked like hippies. I used to look like this in the sixties I thought . . . the black woman said, "But we have to talk about your racism." I was excited, because anyone could speak, and I knew how to speak, from all those years as a Mormon youth speaker, and I loved to speak, and I knew how to move people, from all those years as a Mormon speaker.

And so I spoke, and I said I knew about anti-

Semitism because I was a Jew and I was from Utah. I said why don't you talk about racism? After all, it has no place in the women's movement, does it? Doesn't that make us as bad as the men—to be unwilling to talk about racism? Like some men (I always said some men then) are unwilling to talk about sexism? God, I was good that night. My sister was good, too, she said, "What kind of group is this? It reminds me of B'nai B'rith girls and the meetings we used to have."

Another black woman spoke, she accused the first black woman of being divisive, and all the white and Jewish women agreed. But the black woman named Deborah kept talking about white women and their racism . . . she wept. I felt for her, for myself, as a twelve-year-old Jewish girl talking to Mormon priests about anti-Semitism, it was the same thing all over again I thought, and I wondered if it ever stopped. I was very disappointed in these feminists. I believe I gave them a piece of my mind.

Those women who were there, in that room, were in a mass, and they began to thin out, racing out, saving their lives, until they were only a few left, and they took me in amongst them and showed me how to move my lips and create sound, and they were millions of years old, and they showed me how to howl at the moon . . . they showed me how to clone my own flesh and to recreate myself. They unlocked a door for me in the wall of the basement, and they rushed me and my sister in, slamming it shut, to keep out some of the other women, who began to grow fangs, and salivate, rushing to us to suck our blood, to make us dance as the living dead.

This woman was named Deborah, and she was fat and black and smelled like Africa, she transported us back to the Tigris Euphrates Valley, she conjured the spirits of her ancestors, who introduced me to my ancestors, and there were many of them who were the same. We flew with all of them back back until we met our original mother (the woman who was in *Newsweek*), the one that every woman being can trace through an enzyme in our blood. And when we met her, she took us up to Mount Olympus and gave us axes and shields and our secret and Holy names. I no longer belonged upon the earth, in this world, and I have never been able to get back. For two years, I was not able to walk or speak, for I had not begun to take form again, I was only a glob of atoms and molecules strung loosely together. I was only a cave, a dark empty hole where some seeds had been scattered.

Fortunately, no one noticed.

Everybody's mother was stirring a cauldron, and out of it flew fairies, and elves and all the stories of my childhood. Out of it flew history, blossoming grotesquely into a huge mushroom cloud. Mother caught it in her mighty hands, and dropped it quickly into the cauldron, and she began to stir, in a frenzy, and she continued to stir until it was boiled down, and we were breathless and she produced a loaf of bread big enough to feed the world; and I remembered where I had gone during my car accident, I remembered that I had come here, and I knew that this bread was the bread of affliction, the bread of scorn, but I also knew it was the bread of life, and believed that if I ate it, I would know the knowledge of the tree of good and evil, and

we followed the snake and we went back to where
Eve picked the apple, and we put it back on the tree
and we knew that we could never again leave this
garden, and we didn't want to and Eve told us that
the apple was offered to her as a means to
equality . . . and how was she to know that the
equality offered to her would be in a country that
was not her own, that she would be exiled into
equality, that she would lose her homeland, that
she would lose herself, that she would be cast into
the world of the fathers, as someone who could not
father, that she had thought she was not equal, but
never did it occur to her that equal meant an equa-
tion that went against . . .

I had learned about Myth, I had learned about
myth making.

arc-ed line of white
furious and groaning thunder
rain down to my lips
and my outstretched fingertips shoot electric heat
soaring and I will not cease
erect neck hairs
ions from my tongue gnarled and violent vapor
   rises
for this is my real name:
winding and spiral moment
cracking the everblue
of the sky's eye

And I need to magic to fly
      to hover above the words and the texts
and scream softly down at you
      we are capable of flight, look up—look up

But I am limited to man-fashioned language
  because our language is still a seed-daughter
  itself needing the magic to swell and explode
    in bloom full and rich
  but how to rebirth what has been burned at
    the stake?
and I am prisoner in the dungeon of their
  language
Where is the woman for me to see when I look
  up?
    where is the stolen and silenced abracadabra
      that we need to rise and hover above their
        texts
      and their words
If we were to see one flying woman, we would
  instantly
    know how to rise and join her—
      for she could speak to us in our own
        tongue
        with the magic instructions—

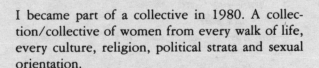

I became part of a collective in 1980. A collection/collective of women from every walk of life, every culture, religion, political strata and sexual orientation.

I was the only housewife and when I came, the factioning accelerated. I threatened everyone, whether from my fat, my culture, my ideas, my marriage or my motherhood; none of which was ever addressed by the women's movement.

I would be seated at a desk all day, running a non-profit referral line. It was the beginning of the 1980s and the voices from the Left were being silenced by the voices from the Right. The voice of women began to turn, as they always have, towards a populist point of view, which again was a voice from the Right. I would sit all day at my desk, taking calls, explaining to women that the information and help they were looking for was no longer available, it had all died due to budget cuts or misappropriations of funding—in other words, Reaganomics.

And I would read. I read the books that sat dusty and stacked in a circular system that Deborah had invented, which she called 'gynocentrific' because even the Dewey Decimal System was invented, it seemed, to blind the eyes of women to our own indigenous thought processes.

I wolved Virginia Woolf, especially *Three Guineas,* about the intermarriage of education, the professions, and politics. Every day since, I've said to myself, "Light up the Windows of the New House, Daughters. Let Them Blaze. Let Them Blaze."

Because we were located in the heart of downtown, we saw it all. First came the wave of mentally handicapped who had been released from hospitals due to lack of funding. Sometimes men in street rags would come in and grow violent. I had a baseball bat to fend them off, and I only had to raise it and they would leave. In the morning we'd find human defecation smeared on our windows.

Then came the wave of prostitutes, beaten, addicted to drugs. They would just come in to sit sometimes, and talk about being on "The Bench." Next came the wave of homeless women and children. We tried to use our non-profit status to open a shelter for them. The response from the women at NOW and all the other women's groups was that we, at Woman to Woman Bookstore, were becoming "divisive."

We did not agree anymore with Betty Friedan, Gloria Steinem, or party politics within the woman's movement. We had seen too much to believe anymore.

Finally, even the books began to change. *My Mother, Myself; How to Dress for Success; How to Lose Weight* and all the regular shit about "how to censure yourself without any outside force at all." *Women Who Hate Women and the Women They Employ.* We began to take to the streets in guerilla theater, disrupting conclave after conclave of women's meetings on Women's History, Feminist Ethics, the International Year of the Woman—all of the circles of the women's intelligentsia and the state of the State which were within our reach.

I had found my voice. No longer wishing to speak in academic language, or even in a feminist language, because it all seemed dead to me, I began to speak as a working-class woman who is a mother, a woman who no longer believed in change, progress, growth, or hope. This was the language that all the women on the street spoke. And I also began to want to speak about will.

We changed the bookstore's name from Woman to Woman to The Rocky Mountain Womencenter. We gave seminars on racism, classism, anti-Semitism, pornography and taking power. At this time, we were plunged into a world of Political Correctness. What was expedient? What truly named women's experience? How were we like men? How would we live with them?

One day, we found another bookstore, farther inside the city. It was a bookstore that sold books about the inner world. The world of will. I began to explore inside. The more time I spent there, the more I realized that the world outside of me was a world I could not control.

This was the final factioning for me—to realize that the way I saw myself was the way I saw the world. I saw myself as powerless, because I defined power as something outside myself. I saw myself as a victim because I could not name what it was I wanted. I saw the world as a place where women are controlled and abused because I had no idea at all of what women's power was all about.

We closed the bookstore down, took all the books and stored them away. We began to turn inward, closing with a circle, and to define the unsaid, the unspoken, to bring forth, to be brave, to tell the truth. The truth to us being that feminism had gone populist, had been manipulated and perverted to mean becoming part of a world where women's voices are absent—because they sounded just like men's voices. Of course, in reality, feminism is not really dead at all. The basics are still all there, right and true, for me, yet I wonder how anyone can see them anymore, when they are espoused by women, hand-picked, it seems, to be acceptable to the Establishment, rather than encourage all women to see what it all really means and how to be able to name it. For without a name or names, nothing is clear and nothing exists.

I began to want to speak about what was between, beneath, hidden. To call it into the world of form out of the world of shadows. I can do nothing else. I never want to do anything else. Nothing else matters to me.

> MOTHER: To give birth to; to create; the act of giving birth or creation (not necessarily offspring). To accept responsibility for that which you create. To mold, nurture, connect with on a spiritual, psychic, emotional and physical plane, and continue to guide, protect and feed. To give form to, to invent, to assume the ultimate innate power of humanity, the act of replication. The physical, personal and political act of caretaking—to bring forth the primordial. To oppose carnage and destruction, to set the physical world right.

> MOTHERHOOD: To put a hood or restraining device around the powers of Mother-ing for political control, gain, and separation from self, to the detriment and destruction of all living things. She Who Is and Is Not Yet.

1980 was the Big Year for me, I had a new house, I was thin, and Bill finally got off the graveyard shift. But inside, I was dying in my mind, in my soul, from self-hate.

Then my sisters phoned me from Salt Lake

City. They were locked in their rooms, from fear
of violence. I told them to fly to Denver, that they
could live in our basement. They came.

We began to tell the truth to each other. We
began to heal. We began to come out of denial. My
younger sister, Stephanie, was enrolled in business
college there, and Geraldine was talking like she
always talked about becoming an entrepreneur.

The three of us were rejoicing in being together again, and we tried to convince our brother
to move out to Denver also, but he wouldn't yet,
he said he would leave Utah someday soon,
though. We knew that it was not as pressing a need
for a male to leave Utah than for a female, though
and so we didn't worry too much about him.

Mostly we just talked, and inevitably when we
did, as we were recovering from being Barr girls,
we would start to talk about our lives and then we
would always get angry and talk about how we had
been screwed over by having to have been born
women. I was about the angriest of all, because
after all, I was married and a mother. Hour after
hour, day after day, we went into intense group
therapy there in my kitchen. We talked the feminine mystique, the female eunuch, the second sex,
fear of lying, etc. Yep, it was a shit-eating world
alright, and it was all men's fault. Bill would turn
up the TV in the other room, and one day he told
me he felt like a black person in a house full of the
KKK. But I didn't care then, because of course, he
was a man, and he was full of shit too.

It was that time in my life, like every woman
has, when you have to throw away the stuff you've
stored in your own head and pick through it, the

time you finally have to think about yourself, not as what you can do for others, but as what you yourself can do for yourself. That is always an angry day, but the good thing is that it comes earlier and earlier for girls these days. I did it at twenty-eight, Geraldine at twenty-three, and Steph at seventeen. I notice my daughter and all her girlfriends doing it at fourteen. I think that is good, very good.

They do not expect to get married and be taken care of forever. They see a harsher woman's world than I ever did, and I think they will be the smartest group of women who have ever lived, if they can make it through the drugs, the pregnancies, and the age they live in. And if they do, then they can turn thirty and realize that nothing is any different for them than for any women at any time in history before them. Good luck to 'em.

But, they all wear crystals, which I feel is such a hopeful sign, a sign that intuition, feelings, and what is thought to be female, the female Arts, of healing, divination, etc., are being incorporated into our consciousness and herald the "New Age" which is, of course, the "Old Age" and for me, the only hope that we will have any planet left to live on at all. I most sincerely hope they will continue to awaken to what is unconscious and not stop at merely having careers. Time will tell.

We admitted that we were powerless over being female and that our lives had become unmanageable. We came to believe that a power deep within ourselves could restore us to sanity.

By the end of 1980, I was well versed and ready to get a career. My sister Geraldine was well versed and ready to get a career, also. Stephanie was ready to get a career. My son was getting ready to talk, my daughters getting ready for school.

Bill was getting ready to kill us all.

I became a cocktail waitress.

I was working part-time as a window dresser for $40 per week and had to get a better job because our bills were mounting up. I went over to Bennigan's and must have sufficiently blown the guy away, as always when processing out loud, because he created a job for me. I was the cocktail captain, a hostess and, if they needed me, a waitress. The men would come in: I was really afraid of men then because I never had had any men friends as an adult. They would come in and it took me a long time to spar with them. First I took all of the horrible degrading shit they would say about your boobs or something, and just store up the info, probably like most women do, just keep it in your brain, like slime and it attaches itself to every cell of yours, like a fungus.

One day something just snapped and I talked back to them. This man said, "Bring me one of these, honey." I turned around and I said, "Don't call me honey, you fuckin' pig." He just started laughing—good thing that he started laughing is all I can say or else I would not have done anything else again in my whole life. So I owe him a thanks whoever he is. I started doing it more and more, and testing it out.

And then it would get really involved. Like the guy who told me, "Do you know anybody that is married and does not want to get divorced, and wants to fool around with somebody else who is married, who has a lot of money who likes to spend it on a special woman and have sex a lot and go to special places and be taken care of?" And I go, "Well, only your wife." Then it started to mutate into a place where you just look at men and you are being so fucking honest with them and they can appreciate it. A lot of men can handle that and that is just always the miracle that amazes me. I didn't expect any of them to ever handle it and most of them do. It's really a cool thing.

The bar was on a platform slightly up above the restaurant, and as soon as I'd take those three steps up to it I felt as if I were entering Rosieland, I mean, I *really* felt like a star. I was receiving all the male attention I had not had in quite some time, and I was receiving instantaneous gratification for it (in the form of great tips). I very much enjoyed it, and my customers used to come in every day. They were these very young and very well dressed yuppie types, with the occasional jock or hippie thrown in.

I owe these men so much, because it was because of them that I knew there was a place for me in comedy. The men were very much like my father in that you could say anything to them as long as it was funny. They would come on to me with the usual male flirtations and I would respond with the meanest comebacks imaginable, but I was learning to be fast and quick, with the constant practice I was getting from eight o'clock in the evening until two or three in the morning.

A lot of the men would talk to me and tell me their problems and stuff too, and I would listen and always try to cheer them up, because I thought of them as my friends. Some were sad, like a couple

Vietnam Vets that were pretty messed up. I would always overpour for them or not charge them at all, and just listen. I thought a lot about the sixties then, and also about my own son, who will never serve in any war (as long as *I'm* his mother and that's a long time). I don't care if the heathen commie bastards are in my living room, my son will never be used as a tool of any government. If he wanted to go to war, I would spirit or lock him away in a room or a country where he cannot escape, because he is my flesh and my blood and I will ultimately pull rank on him, and forbid it. I do not understand why all women will not all do the same. Except I do understand about poverty, and how the army is a way out, and that's another thing that just disgusts me about our country and the world's love affair with war and dying.

I guess all I really want is a world where we can live together—and in peace. I believe that women can put our human race back the way it should be and save it, because I very much want to live here on this beautiful planet and visit my friends and enjoy and respect their various cultures and the wonderful array of food and drink and music that exist.

These men at the bar were my friends . . . They would always laugh and then they would come back and the next time, we would really start to talk, and soon, of course they would be asking my opinions and my advice, and I'd always let them get good and drunk before I told them that I believe they were a very good person, but just needed to listen to women more. I had a couple of them that fell in love with me, but I would almost always say that I was happily married and destined to become a woman that the world needs and would listen to. They would always agree and then one of them told me that I should go on stage. He said that I should go down to the Comedy Shoppe on Larimer Street and let them have it. I said yeah, I should go down there and tell all the men that they were fucking idiots and I was taking over.

I started to think about it. When I finally went, several of my customers went down there with me and cheered me on. So, it was in part because of these men, my friends, that I did say what I say . . . and I would like to say thanks, but unfortunately, I have forgotten all their names (even though I do remember what all their eyes, lips and butts looked like).

Anyways, a lot of them would keep coming in and they would tell me that after they got off from work they would never say, "Let's go to Bennigan's," they would say, "Let's go to Rosie's." And I said, "That is really cool." I would make *50 percent* tips; half of everything I would sell I would make in tips.

One customer said, "This is just like going down to The Comedy Works, coming to see you, except that it lasts about six hours." I said, "What's The Comedy Works?" He said, "It's that comedy club here." "Oh wow, I am going to go down there." I told the lady that babysat my kids that I was going to go down there, and I started all the time thinking about going down there. For a year it was in my head and I was even writing my material, thinking things like . . . "Being a housewife means cleaning up everybody else's mess and it is like cosmic."

I went into the club, I went backstage and all the guy comics were in their corners not talking to each other, and the women were in their corners, and I didn't know that that is how comics are, because I was going into it like, I can and am going to earn millions and millions of dollars because I really think I could, because this is like the only thing I know I can do. I am going to have to learn how.

I went up to all of these comics and said, "Hi everybody, my name is Roseanne and I am so excited, and this is the first night I have been on stage, and I think that I have got a really great routine. How long have you guys been doing it?" They all turned around and looked at me with great loathing. Just like, "Oh, my God."

I went on stage and did my show and people just loved it. The very first night was just great. I went off and the only person that came up to me was Don Becker and he said, "Good set." I said "Thank you."

The second time I did not do well. One lady got up and turned her chair around so that her back was to me, and when I was done there was no applause. So I went offstage, and that night *everyone* talked to me. I told that Susan Bublitz, "I like your act when you say all that about the sexist management. Is it really true here?" She laughed and said well yeah, but I shouldn't really say. She then became my comedy partner; we worked together at the strip club Straite Johnson's where they had strippers and a salad bar in a coffin.

I did Monday at the club for about four months and they would not let me have regular nights when they went full time. It was two comic guys that got together and rented out the top of a bar for comedy night and went all over Boulder and every place with it. They were making guys that were way worse than me regulars. I was very very insecure and I thought, why don't they like me. The audience was beginning to like me, they hear that, I am killing. You had amateurs on Mondays and the guys that worked the rest of the week got paid $15 per show; they opened the show on the local comics' back. They didn't have headliners or middle acts for at least two months—and they did that to their friends.

There was a seminar with two comics from LA, Dianne Ford was one of them; she was a really good feminist standup comic. I talked to her afterward and I said it's really hard for women, isn't it? And she said yeah, it is really really hard. I go, well you know, I know that you are a friend of the owner here and I am like one of the best comics they have and they will not put me on regular, could you talk to him? She said, "I am not going to talk to him unless I see your act." I said will you come and see my act tomorrow night. "Yeah alright, I have to come here and work anyway." I said thanks.

I come in, go on stage, it wasn't that good of a night 'cause every week I was doing a different thing. She came back and she said, "I listened to you, you really remind me of me a long time ago when I first started, but do you tape your act?" and I said no. "Well you need to tape your act and you need to do the same thing every time until you get really good at it." And I go, "Well, that would be boring, that wouldn't be like being a comic then, to just do an act." And she said yeah, you just do an act, because if you say the same thing enough times then you can put innuendo and voice inflection and all kinds of things on it and you will learn how to be funny and you will learn how to write a joke that way. You may find out that raising your voice at the end might get a big laugh, whereas keeping it flat wouldn't. That's the only reason you do that, and then once you learn that, then you can go into more free form, but you gotta get your start that way. I said, "Oh thank you." And she said, well your material is real angry and I like that but you are going to have to work with being likeable. The other thing is that you have got to lose about twenty pounds, your pants are too tight (I was about 130 pounds then), and you cannot look fat and be a woman comic. People will hear it easier from you if you are beautiful, well kept, professional than if you are kind of slobbed out. So the next week I started to wear tunics instead of tight clothes, probably to hide my boobs which was probably a lot of what she meant because eighty pounds of me was all tits. She told me that she would come and see me in another three months and that if I had improved then she would tell George to put me on. I was so mad at that, but I had to do it.

Alan Stevens, who was from LA, went to George and said, "This bitch is funny, why aren't you putting her on instead of these guys, she is funnier than any of those other guys you got." And Susan Bublitz had taped my five minutes one night and took it to George and said listen to Roseanne, listen to this tape, and he did. He put me on regular because of the three of them. He called me in and he said, "You know, Dianne and Alan have been telling me for a long time that I should listen to you to see if you had improved, and Susan played me a tape. I think that you really have improved, so I am going to let you start working Wednesdays and Thursdays, you'll move up to that level." Of course I was the only person who had those levels to go to, but after he had devised that level for me he devised it for everyone who would come after me.

Guys went on stage before me on a Tuesday night and did real anti-women material just before I went on. Like, "I met a feminist and her name was Ms.-FIT, now welcome out Roseanne Barr, a real funny gal." I came out and I did not do good. So he took me off and put me back on Mondays for about three more months.

There was a talent show at a women's bookstore there that I signed up for. The women were sitting on a couch out in the back in the parking lot, and I did my act and they were like, "It's great, it is just a great act, you are *very* good." I was just so happy. I came back to the Comedy Store Monday and I did even better from getting some confidence from the bookstore; I was better than I had ever been and they were very upset about it. They kept telling me, well you can't do this, you can't do that, you are losing the men, talk about more universal things, don't talk about women things, people hate it, get a soap box. Those women said, we have a production company called Black Orchid Productions, and we will put you in our coffeehouse every Saturday night, you can work there in the bottom of the Unitarian church. I was so happy. It was always the same twenty-five women; they told me you have a great show, you ought to go over to the Three Sisters bar because they have a show there and you can practice. I did and the Three Sisters owner loved me; she told Geraldine, "Sisterhood is powerful but your sister is gonna be rich."

So I had two places where I could go, and my routines and I were loved, and then I would go back to The Comedy Shoppe and they would tell me how *bad* I was. I went to the Mercury Cafe and it was all Big Bad Bikers and I would say shut up you fuckin' wimps. I'd go to another place and work in front of Punks: When I did my Jackie Kennedy jokes I'd get a standing ovation. At Muddies, I'd get up in the middle of the Jazz set and open for the musicians, I'd get into the Jazz of words and they cheered for me. Everyone was encouraging me except for the Comedy Shoppe. We went to the University of Boulder to produce the show called "Women, take back the Mike," to coincide with the Take Back the Night march. Always, the same twenty-five women from the bookstore would fill the place and cheer me on. They had all told me that I was speaking for them, I was married and a Mom and people would hear it from me. Their nurturing was the only thing that kept me going.

We went to the local magazine, *Westward,* and

told them, "I am not allowed to work at the Comedy Shoppe, so I am doing this because I am being censored," and all the papers printed it because it was like big news from Denver. Then Ed called me and said I read that you said you were being censored at my club and I resent that; and so I said well, then why ain't I working? He insisted there was no censorship at his club. And then he put me on—but still no weekends. I was a paid comic and I was developing my act very quickly because I could play to a bigger crowd.

In the middle of all of this, I kept thinking: If I keep playing these coffeehouses, I'm going to be a radical comic, but I want to be a *mainstream* comic—or do I? Then I figured out that I could say everything that I wanted to say by being a housewife. I could say, "Why don't men clean things up?" I worked it out with my sister, evolving this character from just six jokes.

We discovered it one day in a restaurant. I remembered my Mom and all the neighbor ladies reading *Fascinating Womanhood* when I was young, and how there was a chapter on manipulating your old man by becoming a "Domestic Goddess" . . . Perfect Wife, Homemaker, etc. I said, "What if I say 'Domestic Goddess' as a term of self-definition, rebellion, truth telling?" Sister stood up in the restaurant and screamed: "My God, Rose, it's Millions, no it's Billions!" We both began screaming because we knew instantly that we had just hooked into the most perfect scam of all times. Sister began the marketing breakdown immediately, as this was her work. Bill even began to believe, and started processing his male-ego shit out into the form of jokes, as this was his work.

When I started doing that act, suddenly I was just so popular. I headlined my very first time out in Kansas City with twenty minutes of an act and twenty minutes of playing around and made $500 for the week. It was the best show I had ever had in my life: I had a standing ovation every night, which I have never repeated because then I was so totally free . . . It was my bookstore act and the Bennigan's Bar act melted into this one thing. That was when I started getting good.

In a period of six months, I had two career choices staring me in the face. I wanted to be a writer, a serious writer, a serious feminist writer, and I wanted to be a stand up comic. I left it up to the fates. I did both, figuring the one I should follow would make itself known to me.

I always do things that way. I read the cards and throw the I ching and then I wait. I was leaning at that time towards being a writer, because Ronald Reagan was just elected, and I felt a very strong need for voices from the left, which seemed to be getting dimmer and dimmer. I thought myself to be of the Left, then. Still a hippie, still believing in the Age of Aquarius.

It looked, more and more to me and my sister, Geraldine, that the world indeed needed to be saved. We set upon the task immediately.

The way we saw it in 1980, was that as women, we were being evolved out of the human race. At that time, we were sitting in a restaurant named the

Gemini, eating salads with lots of sprouts on them, and saying how the modern age, with all its technology, was becoming more and more a cold, dead existence, and how everything that was classically female was being destroyed, starting with Mother Nature. That Bitch was damn near dead. No water, no air, no green was clean. Because they could not give birth, we reasoned, men had decided to try to even the odds, and kill everything. Division of labor, and all that shit, you know. That's what it is, girl, think about it. Anyways, the younger sister, Steph says, "But don't these men know they'll die too?" Geraldine pipes in, "Well, that's what they want, to be dead. I mean, that's why alls they ever do is talk about heaven, the place you go to find lasting peace after everything's dead. Like that's the greatest place you could ever be." I says, gals, "Once again, you only have part of it." (I always talk like that, even when I'm wrong, and Geraldine or Steph adds the missing part. I always act like I'm the one with divine knowledge, and anyways it's usually true—ask anyone who knows me.)

I says they ain't gonna kill everything, they just want to rule it, and whether they're dead or not is immaterial! Then I did an impression of Daddy saying (as he always did), "Do as I say, not as I do," or "because I am the boss around here, that's why!" We laughed and laughed. Then I realized that they couldn't kill everything, just women, that's what they wanted, just the women dead. That's why they were trying so goddamn hard to figure out cloning, cause then they wouldn't need us at all, they could just give birth to their own sons, and have fun little wars all the time! 'Cause carried to the nth degree, which is where I always go, because I'm nuts, remember?, I'm right.

And that us women were being duped, sold a crock of shit, given wooden nickels sister, when we thought for one second that Betty Crocker, *Ms.* magazine or careers, or abortion or day care was anything important. All they do is keep us busy, all our lives, busy busy busy, until there's no more time. Telling us girls that God *maybe* might be a Woman, and anointing a few of us and letting us vote. That only pacified us, let us think we were progressing, while in the meantime, the hugest amount of the earth's wealth was being wasted on weapons. And no, being thin does not mean you'll live one second longer than me, honey. Women, women, awake to the call of the wild now, before it is too late. Any of you out there who know this, and see it too, stop jacking off, brother, and open your fuckin mouth. Say no, say maybe no for chrissake. Ronald Reagan and George Bush and them old guys—they ain't your daddy. You don't know who your daddy is—'cause that's why you're bastards. But you do know who your mother is, and your mother is telling you to put down them nasty guns and shit. And if she ain't telling you that, it's only because she's asleep or dead already . . . JEZUS CHRIST!

Sisterhood's Dead. Motherhood is where it's at. Mothers: make your sons lay down their weapons.

Sorry.

To return to the texts . . .

When I walked into that comedy club on Larimer Street, I was ready to preach. I was ready to preach the word of the Goddess herself, 'cause she was telling me, You tell it, you tell it. I walked in armed with five minutes of material. I performed it while my sister Geraldine sat in the front row, so I could look at her and not be scared. I said:

I went to the library and checked out this book called how to be a comedian. It said that comedy has a three part mathematical formula, and the first part is about the bonding. The bonding between the audience and myself. The bonding that makes you, the audience go "She's just like us, she's one of us, she is us"—but I'll save the metaphysics for another time.

After you bond with me, which you have just done, you will begin to lose your fear of me, especially you men. You will realize that "she's not trying to castrate us, or humiliate us in any way, she is merely trying to be funny." Say it with me, won't you? Bonding is peculiar to males: she's not trying to castrate us, she's merely attempting to be Funny. Say it with me "Castrate."

Next, I will ask the questions of social relevance, and being as this is the beginning of the Reagan eighties, and we're all scared, let's reduce those questions down to the most basic, as many of the proceeding comedians have done tonight.

Why do we fart? Everyone farts, we realize, and now, having been healed of those parting doubts, let's join hands, and with an eye toward the future, promise ourselves that we will never fart alone again, and realize that everyone farts, even Nancy Reagan farts. She farts loudly and with gusto all the time.

Having found rest together, I then move on

to the "bridge," where I form a bridge between myself and you and you form one between yourselves and others, through the gift of laughter, we are now brothers and sisters under the skin.

Well, this is the kind of comedy I do not do. What I do is a brand new thing I call funny womanness. Based on a brand new theory that we women have our own way of thinking, different from the way men think, and really different from the way they think we think. The joke used to be that sex is dirty and women are for sex, so they're dirty, too. But now, it's a new age, and the joke has changed. Sex is good clean wholesome fun, and women are for sex, so they are good, clean wholesome fun too. WE've come a long way Baby.

Let me illustrate this for you by doing an impression of the most consummate male comedian of all time, Lenny Bruce, but first my impression of Lenny . . . hey guys let's all get together and admit we're a bunch of racist pigs and we hate each other's guts. Then we'll stop fighting guys, respect each other for what we are, and then we'll all go out and fuck some chicks, hey!

Let me juxtapose the most classic Lenny Bruce joke of all . . . the Jackie Kennedy joke . . . Lenny said she climbed out the back of the car to get away, to save her own ass, he said this was the human natural response. I'm a woman and I know that is not true, she was sitting there next to her husband, saw his brain blown out onto the back of the car, and she was only going out there to clean up the mess, man.

Us women are all of a sudden smart, over the last fifteen years, they must have put something into the drinking water, 'cause now we're all so smart . . .

During the ten million years before that we didn't do nothing, we just sat there, but now we're all so smart.

Here's the way the commercial should go "Hey Ladies, I've tried smelling like a peach, a wildflower, fruited hibiscus, but it didn't get me shit. Well, now there's a new feminine deodorant spray, invented by a woman gynecologist, guaranteed to drive men mad, it will turn them into raging animals that will fight to the death to get next to you 'cause it smells just like money." See my tits, these are fuckin red white and blue titties, too honey. Big red stretch marks, blue veins and some of the whitest skin this side of cherry hills village. Well, these things are to feed your children. My breasts have fed three children, nurtured and sustained their bodies and built them up in twelve ways. If they wanna lay down after that, by god they deserve the rest. These tits are being donated to Madison Ave. after I die, to help sell cars and stereos and keep up the gross national product for you folks, so show a little fucking respect for me there kimosabe. The end.

Sister and I thought it was hysterical. Bill thought we were. Soon as I told him about the laughs, though, he built me a microphone stand out of an old broomstick and a screwdriver. That's what someone told me to work on that night, mike technique. What a dip, so I did.

About this time, I started going with the other comics over to this coffee house, called Muddys. I thought it was funny, like an Erica Jong novel, that I was here from the suburbs searching for Bohemia. I remember talking to a guy there about the sixties. He was a hippie. He said, "The sixties are over, man, I thought it was just the assholes who were saying that. But it's true they really are over. I've been here twelve years, and I'm goin' back now, I'm going into business with my dad like he wanted me, I lived through all of it and heroin, friends OD'd out and shit. Now I'm leavin' it too. I can't believe it." I said, "It ain't dead, I used to think that, too, but now I'm back, I'm back and I still believe it. I think what happened is that it mutated into the women's movement, all that sixties shit, it helped bring back the female in us all, peace, love, understanding, that's all mutated into feminism now, where it needs to be, because women are the missing piece in everybody else's puzzle. Womanpower is the only thing that doesn't leave ANYBODY OUT, it ain't dead," and he said, "It is for me, I don't buy any of that peace love shit anymore, it's a dog eat dog world, out there, and being into that peace and love shit will get your ass killed."

Well, I thought, "Now you know why women are so pissed off, asshole." He became a yuppie. I still think maybe someday all the old hippies will come back. I did.

What was happening at this same time was at Woman to Woman bookstore, on Colfax. Me and my sister Geraldine went there, when all the punks started showing up at Muddys. The sixties really were dead, I feared, but then this one punk kid, whom I asked right out, Hey what do you people believe in? He said Anarchy and Peace. I said, then let the good times begin. 'Cause I was right there too.

We helped bring anarchy and peace to the woman's bookstore on Colfax, and then we closed it down nine months later. Perfect, somehow. I didn't believe that the sixties were over, I believed they had mutated into feminism, and could not go on without it. I now feel that feminism has gone as far as it could go, and that it has mutated into Women's Spirituality, and cannot go on without that. Some women will stay there, in the world of issues and votes, and careers, and some will go on, to more fully learn the Female Arts, and I am one of those who did. That is what happened to the bookstore, and the women's movement. It's still here, it never died, neither did the sixties, but they're over here now. The New Age is the Old Age, come full circle, the age of enlightenment, Aquarius, and once again we are worshipping the Creatress of the Heavens. It happened, and that's why I don't hate men anymore. This, I believe, is the only way not to hate men anymore, is to not hate women, and vice-versa.

After I realized that nobody wants to fucking hear it, my comedy career began to explode. You could do it in another way, I realized, you could say it in jokes. It was, I still think, the only way. Because the bigger comedy is, the more outrageous it gets, the more you can get away with saying. People will laugh and think you're an asshole if they want to, but you're still sayin' it, so therefore it was possible to say it without getting killed.

When I performed, my sister would watch people laugh and watch how they watched and tell me how they laughed and at what jokes they would put their heads back in fear, and when they would laugh loudly and rock forward, when the men started to let go of their balls. The women seemed so afraid to laugh in front of the men. They wouldn't laugh unless the men did. So if the men laughed at me, the women might too.

In Louisville, Kentucky, I got booed off the stage by 300 college punks at midnight in a Pizza Bar. I had to leave the stage by walking out in front of the crowd that was booing me, and I stood by the door. When they filed out at the end of the show I said to myself in that voice that everyone has that saves your life: "You are going to stand here by the door and look every one of them in the eye and tell them that this did *not* kill you." I looked at the women who were all looking at the floor and not looking at me, and the men who *were* looking at me and sneering at me, and I would say, "Thanks a LOT." If a woman would look me in the eye, I'd say, "You cowardly Bitch, Thanks a LOT." I did that to 300 people.

That night we got in the car with the other comics and they told me, your act isn't going to cut it in the Midwest, people don't like your whining, they don't like your being Jewish, you are putting the men down and they don't like it, they think you are a bitch. I had to listen to their drivel for 300 miles. I said, well what do you think that I should do? They said, just tell jokes, drop that whole women's stuff and just tell jokes, do some fat jokes.

After that week I was able to come back to Denver and do anything on stage because I said to myself, "This is the worst thing that can happen to you and it did not kill you so you have nothing to ever fear again." I went up to Ed's house and started to foment a revolution. It was a great home with a hot tub that he had earned by paying us $15 a night in a club that sat 300 people. He was a comic too, trying to be our friend. I said to everyone, he is making a lot money off of us, we ought to get paid a lot more. Of course then all of them would run to him and tell him everything that I said—boys, you know. So they called a big meeting together to counteract everything. Ed said, "Roseanne, I am looking at this place as college. I am offering you a place to work and you should be paying *me.* There is a possibility that some of you can make some good money when you leave here, but now you're getting a free education." By now I was a draw and people were coming to see me so he had to put me on weekends. So I did start using it as a college: I wasn't thinking about doing a great show but about learning something. I tried my act in a mink, as Moms Mabley, I was experimenting.

And I'd go to the bookstore to test out my new jokes.

The Denver Laugh-Off contest turned out to be sixteen men and me. The guys who were out of the running after the third night were rooting for me, saying you're gonna do it, you're fuckin' gonna do it! We knew that I had won when I picked last place in the draw. After all of their stuff, after the audience had been all the way primed to be able to see that everything that I was going to say about men was true, I could stand up and say what I had to say. This is why the opening act is always so very important.

I went up there the final night. It had been narrowed to the four of us. I did my five minutes. There was a drunken woman in the audience. I got to the joke, "People say you are not very feminine" and she said, "Well, you are *not* very feminine," and Matt Woods was in the back at the bar and I remember he screamed, "Go get her!" 'Cause he knew what the joke was—all the guys at the bar applauded before I even said it. I turned my head, looked at her and said, "Suck My Dick."

And then I won.

After I won the Denver Laugh-Off contest, sister started to bitch at me all the time, "Rose, there is nothing left for you to learn here, go to LA, get out of here. Now is the time."

Louie Anderson started to tell me, "Go to LA, let Mitzi Shore see you."

A lot of LA comics who were working the local club in Denver told me, "Come out to LA, Mitzi Shore will fall in love with you." Armed with all this support, I did venture out to LA, the Comedy Store, hoping for the approval, guidance, support of the Mother of Comedy, Mitzi Shore.

It was a name that every comic holds deep in

their heart. The stories about her were unwittingly hilarious and extremely frightening. She could hate you for no reason, it seemed, or love you, for no reason. She had turned away some of the greatest comics in the country, but by the same token, she had picked out most of the great ones.

Richard Pryor, Steve Landesberg, Tim Thomerson, Elayne Boosler, David Letterman, Sam Kinison, Louie Anderson, Sandra Bernhardt, Robin Williams, and many others whose careers started someplace else and caught fire in LA at the Comedy Store.

Everyone said, Mitzi loves the women, she goes out of her way to develop women comics, it's her thing.

The night I auditioned for Mitzi Shore, I went on stage for six minutes and blew the room away. It was the greatest five minute set I ever had and as soon as I went off stage, the Mother of all the night people, Mitzi Shore, with her signature table-cloth on her head, polka dotted fingernails, plat-form shoes, and whining voice, not unlike my own said to me, and I'll never forget it, even when she drives me nuts, "Go do twenty minutes in the Main Room."

All the waitresses said she had never done that before, took someone from Show Case to Main Room in the same night.

After my twenty minutes, she said, "You gotta move out to LA, Roseann-A, I'll take care of you. You are going to be *the* one who breaks down the doors of Comedy for Women."

I came to LA to rehearse my act for a segment Mitzi was producing with George Schlatter featuring women comics in a show called "Funny." I had no where to live, I had no money, I did have a drive to succeed, and new Comedy Girlfriends like Dianne Ford and Karen Habor who generously opened their homes, couches, floors, and blankets to me.

During the week of rehearsals for "Funny," I was staying at Dianne's. She was on the road working and she left me her little red MG convertible (which I have since purchased from her for its sheer sentimental value). Geraldine was en route to Los Angeles. She arrived at the Comedy Store in time for the dress rehearsal. To prepare for my television debut, Mitzi Shore, acting as both my wardrobe consultant and mother took me out shopping for an appropriate stage outfit and a "Look." I ended up wearing a pair of funky designer cotton overalls because as Mitzi in her wisdom pointed out to me, "You should wear overalls because yours is a kind of 'farm act anyway,' it's kinda midwestern, and I'm from the midwest myself and I know what you need to look like." She bought me some other less formal evening attire as well.

The night of dress rehearsal came. I was nervous, Geraldine was in the audience, Mitzi was directing the "girls," technical crews were being technical, comediennes were being competitive, cuntish, and cautious, each being sure that her act was indeed the best. Pam Matteson was really there for me that night, she was supportive and honest and I liked her a lot.

I had just come off stage when I was approached by a man who was telling me that he loved me. I thought that he was a regular fan, and said my usual. "How nice. Move." He then handed me his card, and of course as I read the card JIM McCOWLEY/Talent Coordinator/ The Tonight Show, I knew the name immediately. Geraldine was waiting for me to come over to her table, she says that she watched me as I spoke to this gentleman, she says that my knees buckled in just a little bit before I shook his hand and left him. That must have been right after he said, "I'm putting you on the show, can you come to my office tomorrow?"

I remember walking past my sister calmly, out the side door of the room, asking the doorman to "Go get my sister!" I was standing in the parking lot of the Hyatt Hotel (the same hotel that I have checked into to write parts of this book) next to the Comedy Store when my sister came out and said "Who was that guy, that guy was someone."

I showed her the card, we started screaming and crying, began running up and down the parking structure, dancing ecstatically for ourselves and our grandchildren, recognizing the moment, celebrating together the impending move off of Lincoln Street, finally out of the Ghetto, the possibility of getting our very own credit cards, and finally our very own bedrooms complete with bath.

After forty-five minutes of dancing, I returned to the Comedy Store to tell Mitzie the news. Geraldine went into the Hotel and placed a call to Bill, then one to our parents. Later that night we drove the red MG back to Diane's house singing both the theme song to the Beverly Hillbillies and a soulful rendition of Eem Teertzoo (if you will it, it is no dream).

The next morning I called Jim McCowley, set

up an appointment to meet in Burbank at the To-night Show Offices. We got in the red MG, we brought the big portable tape recorder with us, I brought my favorite Prince tape too. We drove to Burbank while we listened to Prince sing "We're Gonna Party Like Its 1999" all the way. My name was at the guards' gate just like Jim told me it would be. We parked the car, walked through the building and were directed toward Jim's office. I remember passing the "NBC Commissary" on the way and we both said "O Sis, look it is THEEEE NBC Commissary, we really are here."

Jim listened and approved which of my material I would be allowed to do. The next night I was on the show and the rest is herstory.

The best part of getting on the Tonight Show was that I was able to go directly from the clubs in Denver to a concert tour. I never had to really work clubs and be ground down; they would have killed me, I would've never made it.

I did the housewife thing because I was aware of what was happening at the bookstore and in the women's movement. At women's meetings, I would say that the real power of women belongs to welfare mothers and women in poverty, some-one should go out there and organize the house-wives and the welfare mothers because they are the ones who started this movement, they are the voice of the movement, they are 90 percent of the move-ment. The other women would say, "Well, we would like to do that, but it is not possible." I knew that the movement had turned into a professional, careerist women's thing. They'd tell me Elly Smeal, president of NOW, is a housewife. I said that she was not the women I was talking about, I am talking about organizing working-class women and mothers. They thought they were all ignorant women, I disagreed with them and tried to do housewife material to prove it.

I learned so much from stand up, I learned about discipline, which I'd never had in my life, I learned about language, communication, and writing. I was validating my existence on the stage, you really don't know very well how to be assertive but, in front of an audience, you gotta learn it. I could learn it on the stage, and still not have it at home. When I started to finally make money, I started to get my assertive stuff at home too. The women at the bookstore all kind of told me that I was their voices too, they were telling me that I spoke for them, it was such responsibility, and it was the first time I realized that it was so much more than just me. I got confidence when I thought I was doing it for other women too, confidence that I never could have gotten just from myself.

CHAPTER

21

Hollywood is where, as my husband says, people who were somebody someplace else come to be a nobody. Here are a few of my favorite places to go. If you're thinking of touristing out here, do it like Rosie:

1. Go to Cantor's Deli, order lox bagel and cream cheese, have the Hungarian cheesecake for dessert.

2. Go to the Beverly Center, walk around real fast, since there's nothing you'd really want to buy there, but lots of weirdos hang out there; tons o'teens with moussed hair and black outfits; tons of well groomed homosexuals; tons of yuppies and hardly any fat people, as it's illegal out here to be fat.

3. Drive down Melrose Ave. real fast, as there's nothing to buy there either, but lots of weirdos to look at . . . tons o'teens with shaved heads, mohawks, torn jeans and leather jackets; tons of well groomed homosexuals; tons of yuppies and a black person or two.

4. Drive down Sunset Blvd. and look at the billboards.

5. Drive down to the Pacific Design Center, look at it, 'cause you can't get in unless you're a licensed decorator, and those people there are more thorough than the FBI. Anyway, I went there

with a decorator and there's nothing to buy there, either.

6. Drive towards Santa Monica, where you'll see lots of weirdos, people with perfect bodies jogging everywhere, who turn their heads when you drive by, just to make sure you looked at them, because after all, one never knows if Spielberg or Coppola might just happen to drive by and cast you in a movie.

7. Go to Zucky's deli for lunch, have the corned beef.

8. Drive along the ocean highway to Malibu.

9. Drive Ventura Blvd. real fast, as there's nothing to buy there.

10. Eat at Junior's Deli . . . have matso ball soup for dinner.

11. Go back to your hotel, you've done everything you can for one day.

12. Wake up, go to Cantor's, have lox and eggs. Drive to Beverly Hills, drive real fast through there (and on Rodeo Drive) 'cause there's nothin' to buy there but you can see lots of weirdos; tons o'rich teens in designer outfits; tons of homosexuals in the same outfits, and tons of middle-aged women in the same outfits, with hair styled by Jose Eber that looks like a modified beehive.

13. Go back to your hotel, drive by Century City that's a huge bore.

14. Go to the Comedy Store and then the Improv, laugh at skinny guys in jackets with rolled sleeves, skinny leather ties and moussed hair that say "I dunno" a lot . . .

15. Eat at Duke's on Sunset.

16. Go to Tower records and video, don't buy

nothin', but check out the usual assortment of weirdos.

If you do not take my advice and insist on buying something in LA, you will be privy to the most
mindboggling thing of all out here . . . the utterly
inefficient and deficient thinking of all those chosen
by the stars and planets to seek employment in the
service capacity. I'm almost sure that I heard once
that all of these people come from the same factory,
where they are being cloned and then conspiratori-
ally sent to apply for jobs in order to thwart and
overthrow all that is important in our society. I
can't remember if the commies were behind it, or
beings from other planets.

These folk, who I'm sure are being forced to
subsist on the most meager rations that the minimum wage can offer, are all clad in highly expensive and faddy outfits, along with the required
accessories that we in the midwest and west never
think of, and the pointy-toed boots and shoes that
gather on Melrose Avenue, where a pin made of
old bread dough cost $300. I often wonder where
they get the money, and then realize that since all
clerks know each other (being as they are a race
unto themselves) that they must go to the place of
employment of a friend and then that friend rings
them out on the cash register at 500 percent below
cost (like how I used to do for my friends when I
was a teenager and they would come through my
check line with a TV and I would ring it up as a
$5 purchase). Perhaps this is why they do have such
an extraordinarily hard time ringing up YOUR

purchase, as it takes a while to seep in that YOU are not a friend, you are a paying customer. They always have to do it twice.

Everything here must be done twice as no one can do it right the first time. Maybe they are tired, what with all the sleep they're losing staying up night after night writing those screenplays about life on other planets and such.

My favorite freaks are the heavy metal freaks that pound down Sunset Blvd. on Saturday nights wearing their required black leather and chains, pink hair and black eyeliner, and walk like they got a big stick up their anus. That very white, very middle class walk, that great fear-that-masks-as-attitude walk sends me running for the curb to sit and remark about how those who do not know are always the ones who have to show that they do. It always brings back the memory of myself dressed in hippie regalia parading down the mean Utah streets with a guitar slung over my shoulder, where I would pause and sit on the corner of the very busiest street I could find and go into a riffraff rendition of "Blowing in the Wind" while Mormon onlookers and drivers-by would display that infamous stunned-oxen look they are so very famous for. And after I had seen a lot of those looks, I would rise, having fed, and move on to the next busy intersection.

CHAPTER

22

There really are places in America that have called to me, that make me long to go back in order to complete some sort of ritual that I had once and lost.

Now that I have some money, I decided that I would buy these cities, and their voices and stories, for myself. New Orleans is a city like that. I rented a wonderful house there in the summer of 1987. I could afford to put my children in camp, and Bill was then free to travel around to comedy clubs, and work on his very therapeutic comedy routine. This left me free for about two months, and was my very first time of living alone, indulging myself and my whims, staying out late and having almost no responsibility other than being home at ten every night for my kids to call me from camp and tell me how much they hated it and how very abusive everything was there, or the next night calling to say how much fun they were having. After that, I would return to the bars, homes and streets where I was a sponge and very happily sopping up great ideas and friends.

My house that I rented was pink and hundreds of years old, and under the loving care of some unknown architect had been brought into the twentieth century without disturbing the basic people whose energy and lives had been spent there. It was all glass and wood, and every room had a fabulous "Casablanca" fan in it. You could see the courtyard from any room in the house, and no one could see you, except the very large ferns and assorted greenery that grew there, hot and heavy in the unbreathable outdoors. Beyond the courtyard was a beautiful swimming pool where at night, thanks to my very buuuuuoyant body, I could float around on my back and look up at the swirling Milky Way and imagine all sorts of time and space entering me in a cosmic parody of sexual exchange.

I was very much a night person, and New Orleans is very much a city for and of night people. A city growing and becoming in darkness.

For most people who are of western descent, the dark is a frightening concept. They have been taught to see only with their eyes, they have been taught to sense only through sight and when they cannot see clearly they panic. They've been told that all things change in the dark, becoming frightening, unsafe, larger than usual, and hidden, somehow.

All this is true to me as well. But I like it. I like how in the dark my sense of smell and hearing become so acute, and how my otherwise undefined senses tingle and strain upwards in my body and mind, like magnets, like signals to the darkness itself . . . and shadows become very large and very interconnected and cover everything.

In the French Quarter where I lived, one block off Bourbon St. on Ursuline, there are gaslight lamps, French and Spanish architecture, wonderful wrought-iron balconies, and wooden shutters that split the inside light into jagged lines that cover the shadowed cobblestones; and everything when you are walking there at night sounds like whispers, and

you really don't know if they are human whispers,
or cat whispers, or even if they belong to this night,
or any recent night, or instead, if they are just very
old whispers that were caught in the shadows, to
remain for hundreds of years until your footsteps
disengaged them and allowed them to escape and
take unseen shape. I imagine that they are grateful
to me and somehow close around me for a while
to envelope me in safety. Sometimes they speak
English and you listen, realizing after a few ignorant seconds that they are coming from inside a
house, or apartment, that you are hearing living beings soothing or crying out to each other, secure
in the knowledge that their walls and floors stop
these sounds, that the sounds are finite, that they
do not belong to fat women outside dressed in
black, weeping softly at what she has been allowed
in this great city that seethes with the beauty and
rage of human sleep.

Your eyes became the beacons of your soul
there at night, when you are walking and happen
to pass another person walking, you give them your
eyes and take theirs, and in that quick and silent exchange, you have named and known friend or foe.
There were no foes, as many knew me, and sometimes as I walked by barely passing I would hear
my name, sometimes as hello, sometimes as expla-
nation, and I hoped that it would stick in the stones
and that some other person would release it in hundreds of year . . . ahh, immortality. Out of the
stones came the name Marie Leveau. And here, one
name out of the cobblestones, one name that rose
and echoed shimmering the humid air and slipping
unformed into my consciousness waiting to be dis-

covered at a later, more perfect time, the name
Marie Leveau.

My area was largely one of Gay men, and I
would go to their clubs sometimes at night, to
watch Ricky Graham's shows and be bought drinks
and see smiles and feel the warmth that was given
to me. I felt a city under siege, old and young men
who walked the darkness also, who defied the cold
and terrifying feeling of death that was everywhere, with some sort of strength and respect for
life and art that contained and eclipsed the new
black plague which had taken friends and lovers
and enemies into the bountiful darkness and released them . . . where now they are stories told
and cared for by healthy men whose eyes are
shaded with a different kind of knowledge than
mine.

My friend Otis, who was also my landlord,
would come and get me at night and tell me great
stories about this city, great histories, and introduce
me to his friends who made great gumbo for me
and told me about their grandmothers, who were
Cajun, and here I heard the name again, Marie
Leveau.

Sometimes I would walk to Bourbon Street on
Fridays and Saturdays and just watch people who
were all drinking and sweating and yelling and
stopping occasionally to surround some young
breakdancers, or singers, or barkers, or buildings
while Dixieland jazz blared out from just everywhere. The music in New Orleans is actually something you can hear and smell and see and it
possesses you makes you for a time forget about all
other music, but it also makes you hear all other

music too. And because this is a city of darkness it belongs to the dark people there who create it while the light people passively observe. Dark people have had to watch as light people come to absorb and copy, earning great amounts of money sometimes, especially if their impersonations sound close at all to the original.

But the dark people play on with eyes and faces that know a different knowledge than mine, and they play on with rich sounds that say: I can create this, this is mine, you can listen and copy but mine is the original, and you will never own that. I am so happy and feel lucky to have ears and eyes and great respect for what dark and rich came over from Africa, chained and sold and raped and murdered in a foreign soil, and against all human odds endured, was born was nurtured was saved was kept was hidden and finally was created in this place near the Mississippi River and now released into music that tells that same story to my ears; and here again I heard the name Marie Leveau.

The vestiges of slavery are everywhere, and if you are not watching and listening you will miss them, as they are the core of the real city, and most people are there to enjoy the fruits and spoils of that core, and pretend to themselves that something else, much more civil and white, just made it happen. That is another reason why the light of daytime is so deceiving, you only see what you believe, and you only wholly believe what you see, therefore, you do not really see much at all, if you are a person who likes the light and what is light. I like the phrase "ray of hope" because to me it's something that comes only in the darkness; you would miss that light if you were in the daytime all the time.

Everything dark is quick and unsure and can shape-shift. A pillow in the dark sometimes turns into a body, or a crack in the wall turns into a face, as all children know. They sometimes cry to have the light turned on, to make the crack or pillow become highly visible, to make it static, stationary, tidy. But when I was a little child I cried to turn all the lights out so I could see other things, and I have always looked for other things, and I have always found them too, and I'm not afraid, but comforted, strangely.

The vestiges of the slavery of dark people to light people are everywhere; there are walls around homes that are topped with broken glass bottles so that you could not escape without great injury and where would you go? Many, seeking mystical transcendence in an oppressive world, went to Marie Leveau, a black woman who was a hairdresser, and the Witch Queen of New Orleans, who ruled the city almost all of her life. Healing with herbs and potions, ruling with magic spells, which captured the imaginations and collective unconscious of this city, a powerful women who had learned the Holy alchemist's formula of how to mix politics and religion, thus enabling her to speak several languages all at the same time, who used the knowledge of the dark to wrench some kind of safety for herself and many other black people from the white populace under whose rule she lived.

And when she would walk the street, everyone, including the priests and councilmen, would feel and fear her essence. Behind the statue of Andrew Jackson, across the alleyway from the Catholic church which in our generation served as the home of patriarchal history and politics stands the house of Marie Leveau where her daughters' daughters' daughters maintain her story. I found her tomb in the graveyard by my house—the graveyard that is locked at night.

Her tomb is covered with Xs—the mark of followers/believers—so many Xs—all new Xs—and offerings are all around the base of the tomb— gifts—and I got the thought suddenly—these marks could not have been left in the daytime. Everyone would see—they must have been left at night in the dark when the cemetery is locked up— I looked at the wrought-iron gates—who could climb them? How could they get in? But of course at night, in the dark, who knows? If you listen hard you can hear the whispers of Marie Leveau saying "This is still her city and it will always be."

CHAPTER
23

Well. I'm in one of my favorite moods, when I just get *so* happy. I guess head shrinkers would call it my manic phase—the mind washers that they are, they can't stand to see anyone having a better time than they're capable of having. I really do believe that head shrinkers and people working in the mental sciences have killed or locked away every human being who really did know how to save the world.

Anyways, I'm in one of my moods where I go into my whole magical thinking kind of a thing. Everything takes on like at least three, maybe three hundred times the extra color. I go out sometimes and just start dancing this dance that I saw these black people from Africa do where they bend at the waist and their elbows jerk up and their shoulder bones come out like chickens. That's what it looks like, some really cool kind of dance, that you do in the moonlight—especially on the full-moon night. I love to dance outside where no one can see me (luckily for them).

That's my mood tonight, when everything means something, everything is connected to everything else and nothing exists apart, even me. Every green thing is breathing. You can hear this hum—like when you're at the ocean almost—just a hum, everywhere. Maybe the sprinklers are on—the grass and stuff is getting watered and you can almost hear the drop of the water sliding over the grass.

I feel so hopeful, and alive.

On nights like this while sitting here all cozy on the floor and my legs cropped like Buddhist fashion, drinking champagne out of these real pretty crystal goblets, I go, God, what an incredible life I've had and how lucky I am and how easy it was—looking back. Of course while doing it, it wasn't easy; but maybe my whole life was easy in one way because all the pain was building toward something, and it did build toward something. I get to make up stuff and get paid for it, and get to live like this. I must have hooked into the most perfect scam of any human being or evangelist.

I felt so good tonight that I told my kids, "How would you like to miss school tomorrow?" They say no at first. Then right away they say, "Yeah, cool." I get to stay home with my kids when I'm in this mood, to look at my kids and remember when they were babies, and when they were born—remember their first words and the first time they ever did anything—then look at them now—they're so big, watch how they run around and how they scream, watch how they fight. They have given me good movies.

The kids are all full of all kinds of ideas and help and they're all hard workers and they're very creative—they make things out of other stuff with paste and glue and staples and then leave big messes all over the place and they never pick it up, even if you scream at them. So then we hired a maid who comes up here everyday and picks up our shit, and you pay them to pick up your shit, and maybe you tip her a lot and overpay her a lot. When she can't come over because her own kids are sick, you pay her for the day anyway, because you remember how every dollar is already spent or needed.

In this mood, I think about growing older, and being in my mid-thirties now, and think about how cool it is to be in my mid-thirties. Because when you're in your mid-thirties, you start to realize that this is your life. And it don't belong to nobody else.

This is my life.

To My Daughters and My Son:

I have loved you all your lives. I gave birth to you all, in great pain. I raised you all in great pain as well. Knowing no other function in my life but being a caretaker, being a mother, I brought you forth into this world and gave you nothing. I had been given nothing myself, and longed, always, for something. But I didn't really know what that something was.

When you were young, I came crashing into wall after wall of self-imprisonment. I wanted you to see me strong, so I hid my weakness. I wanted you to see me succeed, so I hid my terror. I wanted you to see me happy, so I hid my misery. In the end, I believe all you saw me do was hide.

I felt that if I could just fake it long enough, it would become true. But my faking it took most of your young lives, and I pray that when you look at me from now on into the future, you will see me for what I am:

Your mother, who wanted the best for you. Your mother, who one day figured out that three pairs of boots and three coats cost $200.00 at Sears, and she knew that she would never have $200.00 to spare, and she could not bear that.

She could also not bear that she could never tell the truth, because the truth seemed so horrible—that she had made a terrible mistake when very young, nineteen—and that your father had made a terrible mistake at twenty. But out of that mistake, you had all been channelled here, and you were the only things in her life that she had ever done well.

One day, I read a quote: "If a woman told the truth about her life, the world would split open." I found a stage, where I began to tell the truth about my life—because I couldn't tell the truth off the stage. And very quickly, the world began to blow apart. Then it seemed I needed to bring your father with me. I could not leave him behind, because he *is* your father, and he loves you.

When I finally saw that your father and I would admit our mistake, I left him, but not until he also had a way out, a future. I loved you that much. I love you now, enough to tell you the truth.

And all the truth boils down to is this: I am your mother, and I love you all so much.

I hope you will be able to handle the responsibility that comes from having $200.00, and the ethics to handle what it will allow you.

Now, it is my time to be happy. Won't you celebrate with me?

Love,
Mom

HarperPaperbacks *By Mail*

Ambition—
Julie Burchill—
Young, gorgeous, sensuous Susan Street is not satisfied with being deputy editor of the newspaper. She wants it all, and she'll do it all to fight her way to the top and fulfill her lust for success.

The Snow Leopard of Shanghai—*Erin Pizzey—*
From the Russian Revolution to China's Cultural Revolution, from the splendor of the Orient to the sins of a Shanghai brothel, here is the breathtaking story of the extraordinary life of an unforgettable woman.

Champagne—
Nicola Thorne—
Ablaze with the glamor and lust of a glittering industry, fired by the passions of the rich and beautiful, this is the sizzling story of one woman's sudden thrust into jet-set power in a vast international empire.

Kiss & Tell—
Trudi Pacter—
Kate Kennedy rises from the ashes of abused passion to become queen of the glittering, ruthless world of celebrity journalism. But should she risk her hard-won career for what might be the love of a lifetime?

Aspen Affair—
Burt Hirschfeld—
Glittering, chilling, erotic, and suspenseful, Aspen Affair carries you up to the rarified world of icy wealth and decadent pleasures—then down to the dark side of the beautiful people who can never get enough.

Elements of Chance—
Barbara Wilkins—
When charismatic billionaire Victor Penn apparently dies in a plane crash, his beautiful widow Valarie is suddenly torn from her privileged world. Alone for the first time, she is caught in a web of rivalries, betrayal, and murder.